Managing Activism

A guide to dealing with activists and pressure groups

Denise Deegan

the Institute *of* Public Relations

KOGAN PAGE

Library
University of Texas
at San Antonio

First published in 2001
Reprinted 2001

Kogan Page Limited
120 Pentonville Road
London N1 9JN

British Library Cataloguing in Publication Data

A CIP record for this book is available from the British Library.

ISBN 0 7494 3435 X

Typeset by Jean Cussons Typesetting, Diss, Norfolk
Printed and bound by Creative Print and Design (Wales), Ebbw Vale

Contents

ABOUT THE AUTHOR

Denise Deegan runs a Dublin-based specialist healthcare public relations firm, Deegan Communications, which she established in 1994 as the first agency dedicated purely to this area in Ireland. Clients include leading international pharmaceutical companies. Denise has worked in the field of public relations consultancy for over ten years, four of which were spent with a leading international public relations agency.

In 1999, Denise received a Masters in Public Relations from the Dublin Institute of Technology, based on research she carried out in the area of activism. Her dissertation, 'How Pharmaceutical and Chemical Manufacturers in Cork Harbour relate to Environmental Activist Groups' achieved a first-class honour and stimulated an interest in activism. Through her research Denise discovered that there was a lack of simple hands-on information for people faced with activist pressure. She committed herself to writing a book on the subject.

Denise has lectured on public relations writing at the Fitzwilliam Institute, Dublin and is a member of the Public Relations Institute of Ireland and the National Union of Journalists. She is an associate member of the Irish Writers Union.

FOREWORD

Even the most casual observer of today's news and current affairs will have noticed the rise in the influence and power of activists. From the campaigners against genetically modified crops in Europe to Internet-coordinated protests against the World Bank in Washington, it is clear that organisations cannot ignore or escape the attention of activists groups if a 'public interest' is seen to be offended.

Considering the above, it is surprising that there is hardly anything substantial written on managing activism from an organisation's point of view. This book fills the gap.

Denise Deegan has written a comprehensive guide on how to manage activism. Starting from who activists are, what motivates them, who they target and what tactics they use, this book goes on to explain how activists should be handled and how they should not. Importantly, the book points out the vital role that activists play in a democratic society and advocates a process of building relationships and community relations, which can act as a positive influence on organisations. It also tackles the harsh reality of what happens when activists will not respond to attempts to build a rapport and how risk in these situations should be managed. The practicalities of planning for activism, media relations, staff training and dealing with emergencies are all comprehensively covered.

The book is written in a clear, accessible way. It has many practical examples and mini case studies and is backed up by relevant and compelling theory. *Managing Activism* is a necessary book for the library of any thoughtful, effective public relations practitioner or scholar.

Anne Gregory
Series Editor

ACKNOWLEDGEMENTS

Firstly I would like to thank my husband Joseph Concannon for his support, patience, advice, wisdom and generosity. I would also like to say a big thank you to Aimée and Alex who helped me keep perspective during times of pressure.

F X Carty of the Dublin Institute of Technology, one of the great pioneers in education in public relations in Ireland, deserves my thanks for his help and wise counsel over the years and of course for his enthusiasm and encouragement of my writing this book.

I would also like to extend my thanks to Anne Ambrose and her colleagues at the Dublin Institute of Technology library who went above and beyond the call of duty in helping me research the area of international activism.

I would like to thank the eagle eyes and eloquence of my good friends Mary Hogan and Eugene Concannon.

A big thank you to those who contributed to making this book what it is by helping to develop interesting and educational case histories – Shanthi Rasaratnam, North West Water; Nick Sharples, One 2 One; Claire Davidson, Shandwick; Alison Clark, DVisions; and a dedicated and hard working public relations person who wishes to remain confidential.

Thanks to the ultra-cool Guy Perrem, of Irish Marketing Surveys for his words of wisdom on research.

Thanks to editor Anne Gregory for picking me up and dusting me off when I was about to pack it in and to Pauline Goodwin of Kogan Page for her helpful advice on publishing matters.

To Robert Blood who provided many useful gems of information as well as a lead to one of the main case histories of the book.

I would like to take this opportunity to thank all those who helped me in compiling my Masters thesis on activism in Cork Harbour.

I would also like to acknowledge the exhaustive research carried out over the years into the area of international activism in particular by US academics James and Larissa Grunig and their colleagues.

And finally to Mairead Lyons, had it not been for whom I would never have taken the first steps down the long and bumpy road of investigating activism.

Thank you all. I could not have done it without you.

Introduction

Environmentalists, workers' rights activists, animal rights groups, human rights campaigners, protestors against genetically modified foods or nuclear power, community groups opposing the siting of incinerators, dumps, factories, etc. Any group that pressures for change can be given the title 'activist group'. While their concerns may vary, they are universally united in their commitment to forcing change. Their campaigns can have widespread implications for those they target and beyond.

For example, Greenpeace's high profile campaign against multinational oil company Shell's plans to dispose of its Brent Spar oil rig at sea in 1995 led to widespread condemnation which resulted in the company abandoning its plans. There followed three years of consultation with Greenpeace to find an acceptable disposal solution. The final decision is estimated to have cost Shell £38.5 million[1] more than what it would have cost to dispose of the rig at sea (£4.5 million). In 1998, the OSPAR commission (an inter-governmental body that regulates marine pollution in the north-east Atlantic) adopted Greenpeace's proposals to ban the dumping of decommissioned offshore installations at sea.[2]

---

[1] *The Guardian* (1998) 'Shell Recycles Brent Spar', January 30
[2] www.greenpeace.org/report98/index.html

1

United States apple growers lost an estimated US \$100–\$150 million in sales at the height of a campaign in 1989 by activist group Natural Resources Defense Council against an insecticide called Alar that was being used on apples.[3] Sales of apples fell by 20 per cent while apple juice sales were down about 14 per cent.[4]

Fast-food chain McDonald's libel action against two London Greenpeace activists, (1994–1997, with writs served in 1991) is estimated to have cost the company £10 million and incalculable damage to its reputation resulting from international media reporting of accusations of animal rights abuse, exploitation of children, unfair work practices and misleading customers about the nutritional value of its foods.[5] Dubbed 'McLibel', the trial became the longest libel trial in British legal history and resulted in calls for widespread reform of the British legal system.[6]

Few will have envied these organisations at the height of their activist-induced crises, yet despite these and many more high profile cases, research shows that few organisations are prepared for activist attack.[7]

In an increasingly pluralistic society, activism presents a growing threat to organisations of all shapes and sizes. And because activists employ a wide range of aggressive tactics such as generating bad publicity, seeking government and legislative intervention, encouraging boycotts, etc, they can cause severe disruption, including damage to reputation, sales, profitability, employee satisfaction and, of course, share price.

Research shows that organisations that come under activist pressure tend to be unprepared, do not know how to respond and either fail to respond at all or respond ineffectively.[8] There is a temptation to bury one's head in the sand and hope that activists will go away. Unfortunately, ignoring groups increases their determination and the likelihood that they will seek third-party intervention from media, regulatory bodies and the government. Fortunately, if dealt with in the right manner, activists have been

---

[3] Center, A H and Jackson, P (1995) *Public Relations Practices*, 5th edn, Prentice-Hall, New Jersey
[4] *Ibid.*
[5] Vidal, J (1997) *McLibel: Burger culture on trial*, Pan Books, London
[6] *Ibid.*
[7] Grunig, L (1992) 'Activism: How it limits the effectiveness of organizations and how excellent public relations departments respond', in J E Grunig (ed) *Excellence in Public Relations and Communication Management*, Lawrence Erlbaum Associates, New Jersey
[8] *Ibid.*

shown to change their approach from aggressively confrontational to cooperative.[9]

Learning to manage activists involves learning about activists. Who are they? What do they want? What will they do to achieve their objectives? And most importantly of all – what is the best way to deal with them? *Managing Activism* is a simple, no-nonsense guide to handling activist pressure. It discusses the various options open to organisations and puts forward a practical, workable, step-by-step approach. An insight into pressure groups is given, revealing their motives and methods. Case studies from a range of commercial sectors highlight both effective and ineffective responses to activism.

Ideally, this book should be read by those who consider themselves at risk from activist pressure as the advised approach aims to prevent confrontation such as a high profile media attack or government lobby. In reality, many readers will reach for this book in a cold sweat as clouds gather on the horizon. In either case, the approach put forward should prove useful.

The subject of activism has been researched for over thirty years, yet this appears to be one of the first books to offer a 'How to...' format to help people cope with the threat of activism. *Managing Activism* calls upon international research into activism as well as the author's experience as a public relations practitioner and researcher in the area.

---

[9] Grunig, L (1992) 'Activism: How it limits the effectiveness of organizations and how excellent public relations departments respond', in J E Grunig (ed) *Excellence in Public Relations and Communication Management*, Lawrence Erlbaum Associates, New Jersey

1

The dynamics of activism

In order to deal successfully with activists it is important to understand them – who they are, what they are motivated by, how they behave and the tactics they use to pressure organisations. This chapter provides a background to activism in order to highlight how disruptive it can be to a wide range of organisations. In outlining the tactics used by activists it is hoped that readers will realise the lengths that these groups can go to and the extent to which organisations can be threatened. Crucially, attention will also be drawn to the fact that the way an organisation deals with activists has a significant influence on how aggressive or cooperative activists will be. Subsequent chapters will deal with the various options open to those targeted by activists and why one approach above all is recommended.

ACTIVISTS: WHAT ARE THEY?

Activists, also known as pressure groups, advocacy groups, activist groups, interest groups and citizen groups, are formed when two or more people organise on behalf of a cause to exert pressure on an organisation to change the way it functions. Pressure is exerted through a wide range of tactics including persuasion, education, direct pressure or force. Based on this definition, community opposition groups can also be classed as activists. Non-governmental organisations (NGOs), such as the World Health Organisation (WHO), while not activists *per se* because they have a broader remit, often function as activists in lobbying for change. However, the terms 'NGO' and 'activists' are often used synonymously.

The majority of activists are single-issue groups, in that they are specifically concerned with one issue, be it animal rights, human rights, children's rights, workers' rights, the right to life, etc. The most common single-issue groups are environmentalists. In the United States alone, 80 per cent of people consider themselves environmentalists and there are 150 major nationwide environmental organisations and more than 12,000 grassroots groups.[1] Two of the most well-known environmental organisations are Friends of the Earth and Greenpeace. Friends of the Earth International is an umbrella group for almost 5,000 environmental activist groups worldwide, uniting close to one million activists in 61 countries with a combined annual budget of US $200 million, employing close to 700 full-time staff members.[2] Greenpeace is represented in 40 countries, with 2.4 million financial supporters and a net income of US $102 million in 1998.[3]

Activists see a problem and unite to do something about it. They tend to believe strongly, often passionately, in what they are doing and can show tremendous determination and perseverance in pursuing their 'cause'.

WHAT MOTIVATES ACTIVISTS?

Activists claim to be motivated by a desire to correct apparent injustices (eg abuse of the rights of workers, animals or humans) and perceived dangers (eg damage to the environment, health, etc)

---

[1] Kelly, S C (1997) 'Environmental Issues in Public Relations: A matter of credibility', in C L Caywood (ed) *The Handbook of Strategic Public Relations and Integrated Communications*, McGraw-Hill, New York
[2] www.foei.org
[3] www.greenpeace.org

for the greater benefit of society. This places them in a morally superior position to those that they target.

As groups grow and take on new members, their motivations can become more complex. Taking on the responsibility of hundreds, if not thousands of members, running expensive international campaigns and offices with high administrative costs, activist groups have to become well run in order to survive. Funds need to be generated and volunteers attracted. High profile media campaigns not only serve to highlight issues but offer an ideal opportunity to increase the profile of the groups, attracting donations and volunteers. When one realises the many benefits to groups of such campaigns, one can see that the motives for targeting organisations can be more complex than simply highlighting issues.

An example of the broad benefits of activist campaigns is the 1989 campaign in the United States by activist group, the National Resources Defense Council (NRDC) against the insecticide 'Alar'. While the main aim of the campaign was to affect policy and consumer behaviour, NRDC's public relations adviser David Fenton has stated that 'a modest investment by NRDC repaid itself many-fold in tremendous media exposure and substantial, immediate revenue for further pesticide work'.[4]

Unfortunately, on occasion, the activist concept can be abused by way of 'front groups'. The motivation behind front groups is more complex than simply raising concern about issues for the good of society. There can be anti-competitive business interests supporting the group. For example, in Los Angeles in 1996, a group calling itself 'The North Valley Coalition of Concerned Citizens' opposed a landfill project planned by waste hauler Browning-Ferris Industries (BFI). It later emerged that the group had received funding from WMX Technologies Inc, a competitor of BFI that was seeking a landfill permit of its own for the region. Creating front groups is a risky business as there is always the chance of being found out. In the above example, when links with WMX Technologies were uncovered, the California Regional Water Quality Control Board found this to be a relevant factor in its decision to award BFI the landfill.[5]

---

[4] Center, A H and Jackson, P (1995) *Public Relations Practices*, 5th edn, Prentice-Hall, New Jersey

[5] Denzenhall, E (1999) *Nail 'Em!: Confronting high-profile attacks on celebrities & businesses*, Prometheus Books, New York

ACTIVISTS: A GROWING THREAT

Activist groups represent a growing threat to organisations around the globe. In an increasing pluralistic society, more and more people are uniting to make their voices heard. Whether this is through community groups objecting to the siting of an offensive project in their neighbourhoods or through the ever-increasing number of special interest groups, the effect is the same - to disrupt organisations. Every day, numerous column inches are filled with David and Goliath stories of how organisations are stepping on toes and how the owners of those toes are fighting back. Organisations are being held accountable. And ordinary people are increasingly seeing a role for themselves in objecting to organisations they do not agree with.

A visit to the Web site 'Norbert's Bookmarks for a Better World' (www.dfg-vk.de/english/mission.htm) shows the extent of activism in terms of the number and types of groups in existence. This Web site provides 30,000 links to other Internet sites that focus on issues such as peace, disarmament, non-violence, human rights, the environment, the Third World, social justice, etc. This and other sites encourage visitors to learn more and to unite for their cause. In fact, there is no doubt that the advent of the Internet has seen and will continue to see a growing number of individuals becoming involved in activism as well as an increase in the number of special interest groups being set up. The recent phenomenon of 'anti-globalists', discussed later in this chapter, is a case in point.

WHO IS AT RISK FROM ACTIVISM?

Any organisation that more than one person wants to change is vulnerable to activism, be it a company, government, church, university, institution, charity, etc. The list is endless. Typical examples of organisations at risk include:

- manufacturing operations, especially those with pollution potential or hazardous risks, eg chemicals, pharmaceuticals;
- organisations carrying out research on animals, eg universities, pharmaceutical companies;

- organisations whose products may be perceived as harmful in any way, eg producers of genetically modified foods, vaccines, beef, products containing CFCs, cigarettes;
- organisations whose activities can be regarded as damaging, eg mining, farming, oil exploration or refining, nuclear power plants;
- organisations that may be seen to be mistreating their employees anywhere in the world, eg through low pay, disciplinary measures, employment of children, etc;
- organisations that market expensive non-essential products to Third World countries, eg baby formula;
- financial institutions that provide funding for organisations targeted by activists, eg companies funding organisations involved in animal research;
- all democratic governments and their ministries/agencies;
- any publicly quoted company is open to shareholder activism.

TACTICS USED BY ACTIVISTS

Activists employ a wide variety of tactics to advance their cause.

Applying direct pressure

Often a first step in forcing change is to apply direct pressure on the targeted organisation. Common tactics include letter and telephone campaigns and petition drives. For example, residents associations objecting to the siting of factories, dumps, incinerators, mobile phone masts, etc in their area can draw up petitions with hundreds of signatures from local people to put pressure on local authorities to refuse planning permission on the grounds of widespread public objection.

Direct pressure may also extend to mass demonstrations, pickets and boycotts. Thousands of customers showed their objection to Shell's disposal plans for Brent Spar by boycotting the company by refusing to buy its petrol. In Germany, petrol stations reported a 50 per cent drop in takings[6] as angry demonstrators picketed the company in an effort to cause public embarrassment.

---

[6] Harris, P (1982) 'Pressure Groups and Protest', *Politics*, **17**, pp 111–20

Influencing public opinion

Activists frequently apply indirect pressure on organisations by seeking to influence public opinion against them. To do this, they use communication tools such as the media, the Internet, public seminars, publications such as leaflets, fact sheets, newsletters, etc. Groups focus much of their attention on the media as a powerful means of swaying public opinion in their favour and against those they target,[7] with environmentalists in particular viewing the media as the most useful tool in helping them achieve results.[8] The more coverage obtained, the more negative the public opinion of the organisation being pressured becomes.[9]

The power of activists to influence public opinion stems from the fact that their activities play on the public's insecurities. According to the psychological model of social behaviour,[10] people fear what they perceive to be threats, especially if they do not understand or feel they cannot control them. Activists work to create threats in the minds of the public, eg the erosion of the ozone layer, genetically modified foods, global warming, etc. Because initially the public knows little about these issues and feels it cannot control them, fear develops, often to the extent that rational thinking is clouded. Then, because members of the public see activists as being proactive in doing something about the problem, taking the onus off them to act, they provide their support out of appreciation and guilt.

Media tactics used by activists

Short-term conflict

Activists use a variety of tactics to create and maximise media coverage. One of these is to 'generate short-term, newsworthy conflict situations to stimulate media interest. One of the most notable examples of this was Greenpeace's campaign against the disposal at sea of Shell's Brent Spar oil rig in 1995 when the world's media enthusiastically broadcast scenes of Greenpeace 'volunteers' aboard what appeared to be flimsy craft being

[7] Harris, P (1982) 'Pressure Groups and Protest', *Politics*, 17, pp 111–20
[8] Dalton, R J (1994) *The Green Rainbow: Environmental groups in Western Europe*, Yale University Press
[9] Olien, C N *et al* (1984) 'Media and Stages of Social Conflict', *Journalism Monographs*, **90**
[10] Blood, R (1996) 'Psychology, Pressure Groups and Environmentalism', *Journal of Communication Management*, Vol 1 No 1, pp 51–58, Henry Stewart Publications

bombarded with giant water cannons from the oil rig. Reports of the conflict dominated international news and the pressure generated led to Shell abandoning its plans at considerable cost. In 1998, the company finally came to a decision to transform Brent Spar into a roll-on, roll-off ferry terminal in Norway.

Scientific research

To lend credibility to their campaigns and to create a news angle, activists often employ scientific research to support their claims, eg 'new research shows that...'. Many groups also employ the strategy of appearing to reveal information that has been supposedly kept hidden from the public eye. This increases the information's apparent significance and helps to present those targeted in a more sinister light. It also helps to reinforce the impression that activists are acting for the good of society. Many groups employ scientists who help both to analyse and generate scientific data. On occasions, scientists can also provide a good photo opportunity, eg 'volunteers' risking their own health to collect samples at high-risk areas such as the site of a nuclear disaster.

Emotions

Armed with scientific data, activists avoid baffling people with details, a common error of those they target. Rather, they focus on influencing feelings by using emotional arguments that appear to be supported by scientific fact. Language is chosen carefully for optimum emotional impact. Messages are kept simple and powerful and are repeated regularly so that they will be retained.

Visuals such as photography are carefully selected to maximise emotional reaction. Greenpeace, for example, used hundreds of white crosses to depict future deaths when it opposed the siting of an incinerator at international pharmaceutical company Sandoz's Irish manufacturing site (now incorporated into Novartis) in the early 1990s. The group descended on the Sandoz site overnight, planting rows of symbolic graves. It was an ideal photo opportunity and media coverage was extensive. Pictures spoke louder than words. People living locally feared that they or their children might become white crosses. People who did not live near the plant were grateful that they did not.

Facilitating the media

Why rely solely on the media 'turning up' to an event such as a photo opportunity, when one can facilitate them by providing photography and/or television or video footage and increase the chances of coverage? On any given day, one can enter the Greenpeace Web site and download pictures relating to its latest global campaigns. The same group is estimated to have spent over US $550,000 to provide the media with television footage of their challenge to Shell's Brent Spar Oil Rig.[11] Footage, which needless to say favoured the group, pushed the story to the front of news agendas, ensuring that Greenpeace messages dominated the coverage. Seventy per cent of the footage shown in the UK was provided to the national TV stations by Greenpeace.[12]

Celebrities

Activists realise the impact that opinion leaders such as celebrities can have when they put their weight behind a campaign. Participation by actress Meryl Streep in activist group NRDC's campaign against the insecticide Alar proved 'an essential element' according to the group's public relations adviser, David Fenton.[13] Compassion in World Farming's campaign against the exportation of live calves took off when actress Joanna Lumley cried on TV about the fate of calves.[14] In May 2000, Hillary Clinton lent her support to the anti-gun lobby in the US, while actor Charlton Heston has been the voice of the pro-gun movement for a number of years. Celebrity objection not only results in wide-spread news coverage but can also stimulate feature articles focusing on the subject being objected to.

Days of international action

Activist groups seeking coordinated international media coverage may designate a day for international action. For example, 11 European Friends of the Earth (FoE) groups took part in a day of action prior to the 1992 renegotiation of the Montreal Protocol (controlling the phase out of most ozone depleting chemicals in

---

[11] Greenpeace media department
[12] Seymour, M and Moore, S (2000) *Effective Crisis Management*, Cassell, London
[13] Center, A H and Jackson, P (1995) *Public Relations Practices*, 5th edn, Prentice-Hall, New Jersey
[14] Blood, R (1996) 'Psychology and Pressure Group Campaigns: Single issue management', *IPR Journal*, January, IPR, London

developed countries by 2000). FoE Denmark held a parade of 50 people in penguin costumes, while FoE Spain offered their Environment Secretary sunglasses and sunscreen. FoE Norway offered their Environment Minister a special suit that does not need to be dry-cleaned with CFCs and FoE Netherlands lowered banners with ozone friendly text in several languages onto a tower at a DuPont production plant.[15]

Advertising

Activist groups often do not rely on public relations alone and are known to embark on expensive advertising campaigns to get their message across. Many will recall the high profile campaign against fur in fashion involving a group of supermodels such as Naomi Campbell featured naked on billboards to show their objection to wearing fur.

Right or wrong: does not always matter

When activists launch a campaign, the media tend to take them at face value, reporting their arguments first, immediately placing those targeted in a defensive position. The organisation is assumed guilty until it proves otherwise and as highlighted in the next chapter, proving otherwise in the face of widespread criticism is a very difficult thing to do. There are occasions when activists can either inadvertently or deliberately mislead. By the time the truth emerges, if in fact it does, it is often too late to save the pressured organisation's reputation. When the Brent Spar incident and resulting media attention had blown over, Greenpeace revealed that some of the figures it had used had been inaccurate. At that stage few people wanted to know and Shell's corporate image remained tarnished.

The Internet

Though a relatively recent phenomenon, the Internet can play a hugely important role in both the creation and amplification of an activist campaign. Immediate global transmission of information, combined with open access by all, including the media, mean that

---

[15] www.foei.org

attacks can develop at such speed that they appear to spring from nowhere.

Activists have taken to the Internet like ducks to water. They see the benefits of instantaneous global distribution of their messages at minimal financial or environmental cost. Like-minded individuals communicate back and forth facilitating the snowballing of issues. Numerous groups have Web sites which interested parties can visit to access the hot issues currently being pursued, activists' views on various issues, recently distributed press releases, etc.

US environmental activist group Environmental Defense (www.edf.org) has developed an e-mail 'Action Network' which has enrolled hundreds of thousands of activists who contact Congress and others on fast-breaking issues. Friends of the Earth UK (www.foe.co.uk) provides assistance and encouragement for activists and potential activists in developing their own campaigns. Campaign guides and briefings, eg The Polluting Factory Campaign Guide and The Incineration Campaign Guide, are available on the Friends of the Earth Web site, as are case histories of successful campaigns. Sample letters (lobbying MPs) and press releases can also be obtained as well as leaflets and posters to recruit volunteers. The FoE site even provides details of other Web sites that might prove useful, for example, in sourcing scientific information to support campaigns.

One of the latest types of activists, 'anti-globalists', took the world by surprise in their speed in coming together in large numbers to object to what they perceive as corporate domination over the world's poor and disfranchised. In April 2000, 603 different groups representing seven main causes (the environment, the Third World, labour, students, human rights, anarchy and spiritual) coordinated a mass demonstration against a meeting of the World Bank and the International Monetary Fund in Washington. The logistics for such an operation were enormous, eg finding places for 30,000 people to sleep. The Internet played a large part in allowing individuals to air their grievances, develop a feeling of solidarity, firm up their commitment, grow their numbers, develop skills, raise funds and organise events.[16]

---

[16] Kirn, W (2000) 'The New Radicals', *Time*, 24 April

Creating media

Another tool used by activist groups to pressure organisations is to create their own media, publishing their own magazines, newsletters and legislative alerts. Friends of the Earth International (FoEI), for example, produces a quarterly magazine entitled Link, which contains campaign news, global action alerts, book and publication reviews and interviews with leading environmentalists. Like many other activist groups, FoEI also publishes books, papers, reports, annual reports, etc. These media can be extremely effective in transmitting messages to other like-minded groups and individuals. Environmental newsletters, for example, have been found to have significantly more impact than the mass media because they reach a specific target group with messages that are of interest to them.[17]

Lobbying for legislative change

In addition to trying to influence public opinion, activist groups may seek government intervention and regulation to force organisations to change. There are many examples of how activists have successfully lobbied governments to enact or amend legislation, from the Montreal Protocol to phase out ozone depleting substances, to treaties protecting endangered species. One of the most proactive organisations for introducing private members' legislation has been The Campaign for Freedom of Information (FoI) whose bills have included access to personal records, environmental and health and safety information as well as access to town hall meetings and papers.[18]

An example of how influencing legislation can work is Friends of the Earth UK's right to know campaign for better pollution inventories, which took place in 1999.[19] The group aimed to ease the process of discovering which factories were responsible for releasing most greenhouse gas and to which landfill sites companies were sending their waste. FoE UK drafted amendments to the Pollution Prevention and Control Bill that was going through

[17] Anderson, D S (1992) 'Identifying and Responding to Activist Publics: A case study', *Journal of Public Relations Research*, **4** (3), pp 151–65, Lawrence Erlbaum Associates, New Jersey
[18] Wilson, D (1993) *Campaigning: The A-Z of public advocacy*, Hawksmere, London
[19] www.foe.co.uk

Parliament. Two MPs (one Labour and one Liberal Democrat) who supported freedom of information then presented the amendments to Parliament. As a result the Government changed the draft law to ensure that powers exist to enable it to gather information on energy consumption and the destination of waste from major industries.

In addition to lobbying to introduce or alter legislation, activists may even take legal cases themselves. For example, in 1995, Friends of the Earth Netherlands filed a legal case against the expansion of Schipol Airport, Amsterdam, on the basis of potential environmental damage such as global warming and accelerated depletion of the ozone layer.[20]

Once enacted, it is difficult to argue with legislation. However, activist groups often find that the wheels of government move slowly, that the standards imposed are minimal and that laws can be difficult to enforce. As a result, they often become impatient and revert to direct pressure on the company.[21]

Hit them where it hurts

One of the latest tactics employed by activists is to hit organisations where it hurts most – their pockets. Activists have begun to focus their attention on the City, in particular the financial institutions that fund target organisations, pressurising them to cancel their investments. For example, in 1999, animal rights activists, Stop Huntingdon Animal Cruelty (SHAC), campaigning against Huntingdon Life Sciences research laboratory, targeted fund managers Phillips and Drew and its parent company UBS UK Holding. Phillips and Drew subsequently sold its 11 per cent stake in Huntingdon, leading to a collapse in its share price from 10p to 1p.[22]

Extreme measures

Certain militant groups, in particular animal rights activists, can employ extreme measures such as threats and acts of violence.

---

[20] www.foei.org

[21] Mintzberg, H (1983) *Power In And Around Organizations*, Prentice-Hall, Englewood Cliffs, New Jersey

[22] Ward, A (2000) 'How Animal Rights Group Hit Company in the Pocket: Pressure on fund managers may have sparked the plummeting price of shares in a research laboratory', *Financial Times*, 14 February

Hoax bomb threats, death threats, arson, damage to property, etc have all been used. In the case of the campaign against Huntingdon,[23] SHAC published the home addresses and telephone numbers of directors of the parent company of Phillips and Drew in their newsletter, saying that it was 'pay-back time' for investing in 'animal cruelty'. Shortly after, Phillips and Drew itself received a hoax bomb warning believed to be from the Animal Liberation Front, an umbrella organisation representing animal rights extremists.[24] Shareholders in Huntingdon have been warned to sell their shares and prove that they have done so or run the risk of demonstrations outside their homes.[25] Huntingdon employees have had property attacked, have been followed home and have received threatening letters telling them to leave the company or face arson or physical beatings. Scotland Yard has briefed staff on how to take precautions.[26]

When extremists target an organisation, the repercussions can be widespread and scary. Thankfully the majority of activist groups adopt peaceful methods of pressure.

Working together

More and more, activists groups team up to apply pressure on organisations. The Washington mass demonstration by 'anti-globalists', The Mobilization for Global Justice, in April 2000, is a case in point. But this is not a new strategy – established groups such as Greenpeace and Friends of the Earth regularly orchestrate campaigns in cooperation with a range of like-minded activist groups.

Many groups such as FoE advise others, such as community groups, on how to campaign, the Internet being a very useful tool in this regard. Groups often lend their support to similar campaigns. For example, Powerwatch, a UK-based activist group originally established to protest against power lines, has broadened its remit to campaign against telecoms, in particular mobile

---

[23] Ward, A (2000) 'How Animal Rights Group Hit Company in the Pocket: Pressure on fund managers may have sparked the plummeting price of shares in a research laboratory', *Financial Times*, 14 February
[24] *Ibid.*
[25] *The Business FT Weekend Magazine* (2000) 'They Know Where You Live: Animal activists have brought protest to the stock market as scared investors ditch their shares in science labs', 6 May
[26] *Ibid.*

phones and their networks. Powerwatch has also objected to a new Emergency Services radio system, TETRA, which uses a frequency of which they disapprove.[27]

FREQUENCY OF TACTICS USED

Arguably the world leaders in research into activism, US academics James and Larissa Grunig of the College of Journalism, in the University of Maryland, have between them researched the field of activism for over 30 years. One of the studies carried out by Larissa Grunig involved 34 activism case studies across the United States, two-thirds of which related to special issues.[28] In the study, all groups damaged organisations with bigger reputations and resources than themselves.

Actions employed ranged from mild to severe with the following approximate order of frequency: media contact, campaigns directed towards legislators or members of the public, lobbying, public forums, petition drives, litigation, pseudo events, public education, picketing, boycotts and sit-ins. Groups began by using mild tactics and became more aggressive as their battles progressed.

CASE STUDY: THE CAMPAIGN AGAINST ALAR

It is useful to review the much talked of activist battle against the insecticide Alar in the United States in 1989, which has been studied by Center and Jackson, to see how various tactics can be knitted together as part of a strategic, well-orchestrated campaign.[29]

In 1985, Alar, (the trade name of an insecticide called daminozide used to slow down the ripening process in various fruits and vegetables increasing their shelf life and improving colour) was linked with cancer in animals. Activist group NRDC led a successful campaign against the use of Alar involving the following tactics:

---

[27] In conversation with Nick Sharples, Community Relations Manager with mobile phone company One 2 One, UK, 20 April 2000

[28] Grunig, L (1992) 'Activism: How it limits the effectiveness of organizations and how excellent public relations departments respond', in J E Grunig (ed) *Excellence in Public Relations and Communication Management*, Lawrence Erlbaum Associates, New Jersey

[29] Center, A H and Jackson, P (1995) *Public Relations Practices*, 5th edn, Prentice-Hall, New Jersey

- In 1986 they commenced their own research into the effects of pesticides on pre-school children. Choosing this audience was a good move in terms of its ability to garner an emotional reaction. Children are vulnerable because of their age and because their parents decide what they eat. Parents encourage them to eat fruit and vegetables thinking that they are some of the most healthy food options. As a result, pre-school children ingest large quantities of fruit and vegetables, both fresh and through fruit juice.
- In February 1989 the NRDC commenced a media awareness campaign, kicking off by offering their research results as an exclusive story to the CBS programme *60 minutes* – focusing on the highly emotive subject of the risk of cancer in pre-school children from eating apples and apple products.
- Although NRDC research focused on a range of fruits and vegetables, many of which had higher detectable levels of pesticides than apples, the group focused attention on apples specifically. This ensured that the message was simple. However, it also added powerful symbolism to their argument in that there is a perception that you cannot get better than apples – 'an apple a day keeps the doctor away', 'the apple of my eye', 'as American as apple pie', etc. Additionally, apples were a popular fruit, consumed in large quantities by pre-school children, especially in juice format.
- The following day, capitalising on the initial shock of the popular *60 minutes* programme, the NRDC held one major news conference in Washington, DC and several regional news conferences in cities around the United States. This led to widespread national media coverage.
- Not simply relying on coverage of the report, the group played an ace card by lobbying actress Meryl Streep to speak publicly of her fears for her own children. One week after the *60 minutes* programme, the Oscar-winning actress called for pesticide-free foods and changes in pesticide laws. Other celebrities followed suit.
- The story took on a life of its own resulting in months of coverage. Consumer awareness rocketed, panic resulted and sales of apples and apple juice plummeted. Schools took apples off the menu. Retail outlets banned fruit on which Alar had been used.
- Activists set up a helpline number. Fact sheets were produced and distributed and a book published.

In June 1989, four months after the campaign began, Uniroyal, the makers of Alar, announced plans to discontinue selling the insecticide in the United States. The US Environmental Protection Agency (EPA) later banned Alar's use on food products. Once the panic died down it began to emerge that the real danger lay not with Alar *per se* but with its by-product, UDMH, which was only produced when apples were processed or heated.

THE EFFECTS OF ACTIVIST PRESSURE ON ORGANISATIONS: RESEARCH

Larissa Grunig's research shows that, regardless of the tactics used, the duration or severity of the conflict, or the extent of media coverage obtained, all activists disrupt organisations.[30] None of the organisations researched felt that they had successfully dealt with activists.

However, it should be kept in mind that while activists have more to gain from their campaigns (eg media coverage increasing their profile and attracting funds and volunteers), such campaigns are not always successful in forcing those pressured to change, which is the main objective of the majority of activists. It is not uncommon for both sides to lose in the traditional cat and mouse game. This fact takes on relevance when selecting a way forward in dealing with activists, as discussed in Chapter 3.

CAN WE INFLUENCE THE TACTICS USED BY ACTIVISTS?

And finally some good news! Research shows that it is the reaction of those targeted that determines to a large extent how aggressive or cooperative activists will be.[31] Specifically, activists often move from direct pressure and lobbying 'to a more trusting, cooperative attitude, at the first sign of the organization's willingness to negotiate'. Some activists, however, will not want to communicate directly with those they pressurise. This situation will be dealt with in Chapter 7.

---

[30] Grunig, L (1992) 'Activism: How it limits the effectiveness of organizations and how excellent public relations departments respond', in J E Grunig (ed) *Excellence in Public Relations and Communication Management*, Lawrence Erlbaum Associates, New Jersey
[31] *Ibid.*

CAN THERE BE BENEFITS TO ACTIVISM?

When under activist attack, it would take an immense optimist to see any good arising from the experience. However, research shows that organisations that experience activism and learn to deal effectively with it through negotiation develop more flexible communications structures in their business generally.[32] Those that improve their environmental performance, for example, have been shown also to improve their relationships with other stake-holders.[33] Additionally, companies that come to understand activist concerns, better equip themselves to deal with other activists in the future.[34] The case study in Chapter 3 entitled 'The Limitations of Persuasion and the Benefits of Dialogue' provides an example of how learning to deal with activist pressure can improve performance.

SHAREHOLDER ACTIVISM

One area of activism that this book does not endeavour to cover is the area of shareholder activism. This is very much a specialist area where shareholders of a company become active against management with the objective of increasing investment returns for shareholders. This form of activism typically stems from dissatisfaction by a number of shareholders with the strategic direction and operation of the company. Shareholder activists are often predominantly investment professionals such as fund managers who utilise their expertise in investment banking, corporate finance and financial communications to enable them to create greater value for the shareholders of a company. What is traditionally termed shareholder activism is beyond the scope of this book as it is a complex area inextricably linked to the capital markets, corporate finance, company law, etc.

---

[32] Grunig, L (1992) 'Activism: How it limits the effectiveness of organizations and how excellent public relations departments respond', in J E Grunig (ed) *Excellence in Public Relations and Communication Management*, Lawrence Erlbaum Associates, New Jersey

[33] Grunig, J and Grunig, L (1997) *Review of a Program of Research on Activism: Incidence in four countries, activist publics, strategies of activist groups, and organizational responses to activism*, Fourth Public Relations Research Symposium, Bled, Slovenia

[34] Clark, C E (1997) 'If You Can't Beat 'Em... A new strategy for advocacy groups', *The Public Relations Strategist*, Spring, pp 36–40

However, there is an increasing trend among activists generally to invest in companies so as to utilise the rights associated with shareholdings to try to influence those organisations. This too can be termed shareholder activism; however, it is very much part of the general activist domain and will be covered by the general recommendations in this book.

SUMMARY

- Activists represent a growing threat to organisations in an increasingly pluralistic society.
- They use a wide range of tactics including direct pressure on those targeted as well as seeking media, public, regulatory and government intervention. More recently activists are targeting financial institutions that fund certain organisations.
- Regardless of the tactics used or the length or severity of the resulting conflict, activists disrupt those they target.
- It is the reaction of the organisation to a large extent that determines how aggressive or cooperative activists will be.
- Activists are more likely to cooperate with organisations that are open to negotiation.
- Organisations that learn how to deal effectively with activists improve their functioning in a broader sense.

2

How not to deal with activists

When deciding how to respond to activist pressure, organisations may consider various approaches, including:

1. simply ignoring activists;
2. ignoring them but seeking to influence public opinion;
3. seeking to mislead audiences;
4. persuading activists of the organisation's position;
5. fighting back.

This chapter discusses the limitations to each of these approaches.

IGNORING ACTIVISTS

Ignoring activists tends to be the most common response to activist pressure. There are many reasons for this approach:

● Management may not know how to respond and fear making costly mistakes – the 'better to do nothing than put my foot in it' approach.

- There may be a belief that there is little one can do to respond because, for example, activists' claims may be true or close to the truth.
- Some organisations do not respond for fear of being perceived as bullies by fighting back.
- There may be an assumption that the public will not believe activists.
- Organisations often underestimate the power of activists.
- Many believe that responding to activists increases the legitimacy of groups.
- Some simply hope that activists will eventually lose interest and go away.

Ignoring activists tends to be a knee-jerk response by those feeling the heat rather than a proactive and pre-planned strategy. In fact, if one is honest, many of the 'reasons' given by organisations for not responding to activists are in reality excuses for inaction.

Heads down organisations try to carry on business as usual, ignoring the existence of groups and their demands. However, it is far from 'business as usual' as activists, viewing organisations as stonewalling, seek third-party intervention from media and government to force change. As public pressure mounts, the targeted organisation is forced to react or risk its reputation, sales, share price, employee satisfaction, etc.

Damage limitation exercises have to be instigated and resources diverted to problem solving as a matter of urgency. And because they get dragged into the conflict only when they can no longer avoid it, they discover that influencing public opinion has become a mammoth task. Audiences will have been bombarded with powerful messages from activists and are likely to have made up their minds against the organisation.

Ignoring activists therefore effectively hands control over to groups, allowing issues to spiral out of control. Whatever their reason for ignoring activists, members of management should ask themselves if they can afford to ignore groups. The case of Nike and workers' rights activists, as studied by Seymour and Moore,[1] highlights the danger of allowing issues to escalate.

---

[1] Seymour, M and Moore, S (2000) *Effective Crisis Management*, Cassell, London

CASE STUDY: NIKE LANDS IN HOT WATER – PART 1

During the summer of 1996, a host of workers' rights and human rights groups targeted leading sports shoe manufacturer, Nike, alleging that it was mistreating its workforce in Asia. Nike was just one of many companies accused of running 'sweatshops' in the Far East. Yet despite a high level of public and government concern on the issue, Nike, one of the world's most popular brands, surprised the world by its response.

The company refused to speak with activists and ignored their calls for independent monitoring of its Asian factories. Nike claimed that because subcontractors ran the factories and not Nike *per se*, the company had little influence. Nike sought to distance itself from the crisis, limiting its response to setting up its own 'Labour Practices Department'.

Nike's refusal to meet groups increased their suspicions and rein-forced their commitment for independent monitoring of factories.[2] Jeff Ballinger, founder of activist group Press For Change,[3] has said, 'Nike has been the most arrogant company involved in this issue. Even when they were caught red-handed, it took them years to address the concerns. At least other companies apologised for their actions'.

Unhappy with the response from Nike, groups embarked on a campaign to make life so uncomfortable for the company that it would have to change. A major feature of this campaign involved the screening, in October 1996, of a CBS television programme *48 Hours* that reported on Nike's work practices in Asia. Nike's managers remained tight-lipped as terrified workers spoke of their personal experiences. Following the programme, a factory worker from one of Nike's Asian factories toured the United States speaking of her experiences and those of her colleagues publicly and to the media. A media frenzy followed and the story took on a life of its own. For the next two years, report after report accused Nike of human rights violations and unfair labour practices.

Nike's stores were picketed. Student organisations pressured their colleges to boycott Nike's contracts for sportswear. Activist groups (such as 'Justice! Do It Nike Boycott Group') and Web sites (such as 'Boycott Nike', 'Praying for Nike's Soul' and 'Nike Campaign') were set up specifically targeting the company. The media condemned Nike-sponsored sports stars for their involvement with the company and US politicians applied direct pressure to the company to improve its work practices in Asia.

---

[2] Boulding, W, *The Reapolitik of Shilling Shoes*, www.geocities.com/Athens/Acropolis/5232/ne-nike2.html
[3] *Ibid.*

IGNORING GROUPS BUT SEEKING TO INFLUENCE PUBLIC OPINION

Some organisations respond to activist pressure by ignoring groups but seeking to influence public opinion in response to criticism. This is usually attempted through the media. In theory, this would seem a reasonable approach. In practice, however, changing people's attitudes and behaviour is very difficult even at the best of times when an organisation is not coming under attack from activists. As Wilcox and his colleagues explain:[4]

> ... the effectiveness of persuasive techniques is greatly exaggerated. Persuasion is not an exact science, and no surefire way exists to predict that people will be persuaded to believe a message or act on it. If persuasive techniques were as refined as the critics say, all people might be driving the same make of automobile, using the same soap, and voting for the same political candidate.

In trying to persuade public opinion, organisations have to contend with the fact that their messages are unlikely to reach all intended audiences and, of those reached, people holding opposing views are likely to dismiss the message as either wrong or biased.[5] To compound the situation, when an organisation is coming under attack from activists, people who have no set views of the organisation are being exposed to competing messages from activists – messages that are emotive and anti-organisation. Every time the organisation tries to put forward its view in the media, activists counter it resulting in a tit-for-tat battle through the media. As Grunig and Hunt explain:[6] 'The result is that a lot of accurate, but incomplete, information is publicized, and publics do not get enough information to make reasonable decisions about new technology such as nuclear power'.

Many organisations whose initial response is to ignore groups subsequently progress to trying to influence public opinion as they come under unrelenting attack.

---

[4] Wilcox, D L *et al* (1997) *Public Relations Strategies and Tactics*, 5th edn, Longman, New York

[5] *Ibid.*

[6] Grunig, J and Hunt, T (1984) *Managing Public Relations*, Holt, Rinehart & Winston, Forth Worth, TX

CASE STUDY: NIKE LANDS IN HOT WATER – PART 2

Nike, seeking to influence public opinion, placed full-page newspaper advertisements reporting the findings of an independent, Nike-commissioned inspection into 15 of its Asian factories in 1997. However, its efforts to reassure the public backfired. As soon as the advertisements were published, the media, who had begun investigations of their own, rubbished the report, questioned its independence and highlighted abuses that they had uncovered at the time the investigation was taking place.

Only months later, a concerned Nike employee leaked the results of another independent report that had been commissioned by the company but had been kept under wraps. It drew attention to worrying conditions at the company's Vietnam operations such as the exposure of workers in one plant to carcinogens far exceeding local legal limits, where over three-quarters of the workforce had developed breathing problems and employees had to work 65 hours a week for US $10. Further negative publicity and accusations of a cover-up resulted. Nike tried in vain to persuade audiences that things had improved since the report had been carried out. However, when questioned, they admitted that they had not checked to see if chemical levels met legal limits.

The pressure on Nike only began to ease after two years when it embarked on a genuine programme to improve work practices at its Asian plants and to make itself more accountable. The company introduced independent monitoring programmes, adopted US occupational safety standards overseas, increased the minimum age of footwear factory workers to 18, introduced educational programmes at factories and funded research into global manufacturing and responsible business practices. In conjunction with a Colorado-based interest group, Vietnam Women's Union, it set up a programme to support Vietnamese women to create small businesses. Nike promised to terminate contracts with subcontractors who were found to carry out abuses.

Only when Nike acted to improve the situation did pressure ease. These actions could have been taken much earlier in negotiation with activists, saving the company much embarrassment, grief and expense. At the height of the crisis, Nike experienced overall financial losses for the first time in 13 years. However, other factors such as a recession in Asia and a fall in popularity of sports shoes are also likely to have had an impact.[7]

---

[7] Seymour, M and Moore, S (2000) *Effective Crisis Management*, Cassell, London

SEEKING TO MISLEAD AUDIENCES

Some organisations may seek to mislead the public about the true situation. In the short term this may work to ease concerns. However, in the long run the truth has a tendency to out and when it does, the result is usually considerably worse, as the organisation is regarded as untrustworthy and deceitful. The truth can emerge in many ways including the following:

- concerned or disgruntled employees, ex-employees, directors, etc of the organisation or its agents may leak the information;
- activists may uncover the truth through their investigations (which may involve 'moles' within the organisation) and go public;
- investigative reporters may uncover the truth;
- internal documents that have not been disposed of correctly may fall into the wrong hands;
- court cases and legal proceedings uncover all sorts of interesting information that the company can no longer keep hidden.

TRYING TO PERSUADE ACTIVISTS

If ignoring activists has limited effects, it would seem a step forward to communicate directly with them to persuade them of the organisation's side of the story.

The limitations of persuasion have already been referred to in this chapter. Unfortunately, trying to persuade activists is considerably more difficult than trying to influence public opinion, as activists are suspicious of, and do not trust, the organisations they are pressurising.

Approaching activists with the sole purpose of trying to persuade them of the organisation's way of thinking is likely to be ineffective and may in fact have the opposite effect. Anderson's case history outlined in Chapter 3 highlights the futility of trying to persuade activists.

FIGHTING BACK

When under attack from activists, there may be a strong temptation to fight back. Options include trying to discredit groups publicly, initiating lawsuits against them or seeking to undermine their funding.

In considering this approach, organisations should bear in mind that keeping activists quiet is likely to be extremely time-consuming and expensive and has limited chances of success. Groups tend to prosper when threatened, becoming more determined than ever. The media, who love David and Goliath stories, always side with David. This increases public sympathy, boosting donations and volunteers to the group. Morale at the organisation is affected and loyal customers may turn to competitors. Ultimately there is a need to question the return on such an investment compared with similar resources invested in improving the overall operation in negotiation with groups.

Fast-food chain McDonald's learnt the risks associated with responding aggressively to activist pressure the hard way when it brought two environmentalists to court in the early 1990s. The case is followed in detail in an insightful book entitled *McLibel: Burger culture on trial*.[8]

CASE STUDY: McDONALD'S, McLIBEL, McSPOTLIGHT

In 1990, fast-food chain McDonald's served libel writs on five environmentalists connected with a group called London Greenpeace (unconnected with international environmental group Greenpeace) on the basis of a leaflet entitled *What's Wrong With McDonald's?*. The leaflet, produced by London Greenpeace, accused McDonald's of damaging the environment, cruelty to animals, promoting an unhealthy diet, exploiting children and treating staff unfairly. Under threat of legal action, three of the activists publicly apologised; however, two, Helen Steele and Dave Morris, refused and the action went ahead against them. The trial, dubbed 'McLibel', which began in June 1994, was to turn into the longest civil trial in British legal history. The final verdict was read in June 1997. 'McLibel' is estimated to have cost McDonald's £10 million.

The story of the world's largest food retailer using British libel laws against two unwaged critics with no access to free legal aid,

---

[8] Vidal, J (1997) *McLibel: Burger culture on trial*, Pan Books, London

attracted intense, ongoing, international media interest and wide-spread anti-McDonald's demonstrations. Though technically McDonald's won on legal points, they lost the public relations battle as the presiding judge found against the company for exploiting children, cruelty to animals, unfair work practices and low pay in its British operation, being strongly antipathetic to the unionisation of restaurant workers and misleading customers on the nutritional value of their food. Though the defendants were fined £60,000 for libels in the leaflet, they considered the ruling a victory and never paid the damages.

If it was McDonald's intention to quieten critics, their writ failed. The 'McLibel' case resulted in significantly more widespread coverage than London Greenpeace could ever have achieved with their leaflets alone. Intense media interest followed the long drawn-out trial and the final ruling was front-page news. The defendants and growing ranks of supporters fought McDonald's vigorously. Steele and Morris countersued the company and a wide range of protests followed the trial including:

- 'Operation Send-It-Back': launched in October 1994 by the McLibel Support Campaign. Fifty protesters returned 30 sacks of McDonald's litter picked up from the streets.
- National March Against McDonald's: held in October 1994 in central London. Five hundred demonstrators took to the streets.
- 10th, 11th and 12th Annual Worldwide Days of Action Against McDonald's: October 1994, 1995, 1996. Worldwide protests.
- Demonstrations to mark the 40th Birthday of McDonald's: April 1995. Worldwide demonstrations in 20 countries.
- Boycotting McDonald's TV advertisement: June 1995. Shooting for a television advertisement in London had to be abandoned at a cost of £100,000 as protesters continuously jumped in front of the camera with 'McGreedy' banners.
- Days of Solidarity with McDonald's Workers in the UK: October 1995 and 1996. Protests to mark the 3rd and 4th anniversaries of the death of a McDonald's employee who died of electrocution at a McDonald's outlet in Manchester.
- Launch of 'McSpotlight Web site': February 1996, launched by defendants outside a McDonald's store in central London. In its first year, the site was accessed over seven million times.
- Second anniversary of 'McLibel': June 1996. Picket outside the court featuring a cake of a not-so-happy Ronald McDonald.
- 'McLibel Gathering (Mobilise Against Big Mac)': September 1996. Workshops on the anti-McDonald's campaign.
- 'Victory Day of Action': 21st June 1997: Two days after the final

verdict was read, thousands of protesters in at least 13 countries distributed hundreds of thousands more 'What's Wrong With McDonald's?' leaflets at McDonald's outlets.

- Full-length documentary: '*McLibel: Two worlds collide*' produced and videos made available.
- The court ruling provided fuel for other pressure groups to target McDonald's including animal rights activists, labour activists, trade unions and local residents' associations objecting to the opening of new stores in their area.

After the final verdict was read, a four-week period was allocated to allow for further applications. McDonald's failed to take further legal action within this period, effectively abandoning efforts to stop further distribution of the leaflets or to collect legal costs. The company said that it would not attempt to collect damages.[9]

McDonald's experience highlights the risks associated with taking activists to court. However, there may still be people who consider silencing critics to be the most effective option. The following case study highlights just what lengths may be required to achieve this (if in fact it can be achieved) and the public criticism that can be attracted should such tactics come to light.

CASE STUDY: TIMBERLANDS FAILS TO 'NEUTRALISE' CRITICS

In 1991, Timberlands West Coast Ltd, a logging company owned by the New Zealand government, embarked on a campaign to 'neutralise' opponents to their rainforest logging. In order to achieve this, an ever-increasing range of costly tactics became necessary over an eight-year period, including:[10]

- attempting to discredit and marginalise opponents publicly;
- sending 'moles' to attend meetings of conservation groups to source information that might discredit groups and individuals;
- photographing and videotaping participants in anti-logging protests;
- threatening protesters with legal action;
- seeking to identify financial weaknesses in one of its most long-standing critics, The Royal Forest and Bird Protection Society (F&B);

---

[9] Vidal, J (1997) *McLibel: Burger culture on trial*, Pan Books, London

[10] Hager, N and Burton, B (1999) *Secrets and Lies: The anatomy of an anti-environmental PR campaign*, Craig Potton Publishing, Nelson, New Zealand

- attempting to undermine activist group Native Forest Action's sources of funding;
- screening journalists who wrote unfavourable articles and applying pressure to stop further articles by, for example, complaining to their editors;
- putting pressure on an environmentalist academic who opposed them by complaining to the vice-chancellor of her university;
- writing to school principals whose students had been involved in a peaceful protest against Timberlands, threatening legal action in the advent of any further protests;
- creating a community front group, 'Coast Action Network' that would appear to represent the voice of the local community;
- developing a system whereby local residents would sign letters to the editor drafted by company advisors in response to negative news coverage or letters;
- exaggerating the number of local people employed in logging;
- physically destroying a treetop protest of a small group of Native Forest Action supporters by helicopter;
- repeatedly removing anti-Timberlands graffiti, which kept reappearing;
- attempting to split the concerns of environmental groups.

The multimillion-dollar campaign was still ongoing in 1999 when an insider who had become uncomfortable with the tactics employed leaked confidential internal documents. This led to the publication of a book detailing the campaign, *Secrets and Lies: The anatomy of an anti-environmental PR campaign*.[11] There followed a public outcry and political turmoil as New Zealand's then Prime Minister was linked to the scandal. She was defeated at the next elections in November 1999. The first act of the new government was to demand that Timberlands cancel a planning hearing that had been scheduled for the following week. Thereafter negotiations followed about ending the company's other native logging.

DO NOT DO WHAT YOU WOULD NOT WANT TO BE SEEN DOING

It may sound obvious, but if an organisation finds that it is being secretive about activities it is carrying out, there is usually good

---

[11] Hager, N and Burton, B (1999) *Secrets and Lies: The anatomy of an anti-environmental PR campaign*, Craig Potton Publishing, Nelson, New Zealand

reason, for example there may be a risk of public condemnation should these activities be revealed. Apart from the obvious fact that ethical behaviour is always desirable, organisations also need to be aware that there is always a risk that the public will find out if they are behaving unethically.

As can be seen from two case histories in this chapter (Nike and Timberlands), employees who are unhappy about organisational activities have a tendency to do something about it eventually, such as leaking information on these activities to activists or the media. It is a good guide to avoid carrying out activities that would damage the organisation's reputation if they were to be made public.

HOW ORGANISATIONS DEAL WITH ACTIVISTS: RESEARCH

Larissa Grunig's research into activism[12] has shown how organisations tend to react in the face of activist pressure. Of the 34 owners of organisations interviewed, most (22) ignored input from not only activists but also from associates and employees. Even those faced with powerful groups that had the sympathy of the media or government agencies still risked ignoring demands.

Of those that did respond to activist pressure, the most common approach was to 'gather intelligence'. Some organisations ignored activists but sought to influence public opinion. Few organisations compromised; however, those that did deemed the results to be positive. In all other situations the organisations suffered, the biggest costs being negative public opinion and government regulation, in order of importance.

SUMMARY

- Ignoring activists increases the likelihood that they will seek third-party intervention from the media, the government and

---

[12] Grunig, L (1992) 'Activism: How it limits the effectiveness of organizations and how excellent public relations departments respond', in J E Grunig (ed), *Excellence in Public Relations and Communication Management*, Lawrence Erlbaum Associates, New Jersey

the public to force change. Avoiding issues encourages them to spiral out of control.

- Seeking to influence public opinion in response to activist pressure is extremely difficult as people's behaviour and attitudes are hard to change especially in turbulent environments.
- Aggressive behaviour such as trying to discredit groups publicly, initiating lawsuits against them or seeking to undermine their funding is likely to require endless financial and human resources. Groups prosper when threatened and an organisation's reputation can be badly damaged by being publicly presented as a bully.
- Seeking to persuade activists of 'the bigger picture' has limited effect as activists resist being persuaded.
- International research shows that the above responses have limited effect.

3

A way forward

As we have learnt in the previous chapter, reactive approaches to dealing with activists such as ignoring them, opposing them or even trying to persuade them or the public of the organisation's side of the story have limited effect and may in fact worsen the situation. This chapter discusses a way forward that involves proactively working with activists to avoid conflict. Chapter 7 deals with the eventuality that some activist groups may not want to work with organisations.

NOT POLES APART

Activists tend not to trust the organisations they target, considering them corrupt, inept, uncooperative or unresponsive.[1] On the other side of the fence, organisations tend to consider activists as misinformed and trouble making. Research shows that because both sides avoid dialogue they fail to realise that their views are not as opposed as either side assumes.[2] Importantly, research also

---

[1] Browne, W P (1985) 'Variations in the Behaviour and Style of State Lobbyists and Interest Groups', *Journal of Politics*, **47**, pp 450–68
[2] Grunig, J and Grunig, L (1997) *Review of a Program of Research on Activism: Incidence in four countries, activist publics, strategies of activist groups, and organizational responses to activism*, Fourth Public Relations Research Symposium, Bled, Slovenia

shows that once activists realise that organisations are willing to negotiate, they become less aggressive and less likely to involve third parties.[3]

PROACTIVE DIALOGUE, NEGOTIATION AND CONFLICT RESOLUTION

As reactive approaches to activism have limited effect, a more proactive approach involving negotiation and conflict resolution, known as 'two-way symmetrical communications', should be considered. This involves learning as much as possible about activists and seeking to initiate two-way dialogue with them with a view to working together on an ongoing basis to reach a situation that benefits both parties. Central to the two-way communications process is relationship building and an acceptance that compromise on both sides may be necessary. The organisation must be prepared to change aspects of the way it functions in response to what it learns, while activists may also need to compromise on their expectations. Only in working closely together can a mutually beneficial situation result.

HOW ORGANISATIONS CAN BENEFIT FROM WORKING WITH ACTIVISTS

For many organisations, embarking on a course of two-way symmetrical communications with activists will involve a change of mindset as compromise is often regarded as a sign of failure. For this reason, there is a need to explore the potential benefits of two-way symmetrical programmes:

- Relationship building allows direct access to the changing views of activists and potential activists. This facilitates quick and proactive response and adaptation.
- Being proactive increases control over potential threats.

---

[3] Grunig, L (1992) 'Activism: How it limits the effectiveness of organizations and how excellent public relations departments respond', in J E Grunig (ed) *Excellence in Public Relations and Communication Management*, Lawrence Erlbaum Associates, New Jersey

- Cooperating means that activists are less likely to seek third-party intervention from the media, government and regulatory authorities.
- The organisation can genuinely improve the way it performs and be recognised as doing so by activists without having to persuade.
- Improving performance helps to improve relations, not only with activists, but also with other stakeholders in the organisation.[4]
- Because of their direct experience of the organisation's openness and genuine efforts to improve performance, activists are more likely to trust it in the event of an emergency, such as a chemical spill.

As highlighted by the Nike and Shell case histories in the previous chapter, compromise is often forced on organisations at the end of an embarrassing public campaign. As outlined above, however, there are benefits to be obtained from taking a proactive decision to be open to compromise as part of a negotiation process with activists aimed at avoiding conflict and its negative impact (eg damage to reputation, introduction of constricting legislation, etc).

CAN ACTIVISTS BENEFIT FROM WORKING WITH ORGANISATIONS?

While activist campaigns disrupt those they target, they do not necessarily result in the achievement of their goal of forcing change – organisations may continue to behave in the same way they did prior to being targeted. Activists have no guarantee that their campaigns will work despite significant financial and human resource investment. However, two-way symmetrical communications with an organisation offers:

- a commitment by the organisation to improve;
- an opportunity to take part in facilitating that improvement;

---

[4] Grunig, J and Grunig, L (1997) *Review of a Program of Research on Activism: Incidence in four countries, activist publics, strategies of activist groups, and organizational responses to activism,* Fourth Public Relations Research Symposium, Bled, Slovenia

- minimal investment of resources compared with instigating and maintaining campaigns;
- a potentially more speedy resolution;
- an argument against critics accusing the group of being unco-operative;
- if progress is not made, the group can always cease relations without having invested significant resources.

US environmental group Environmental Defense Fund regularly works with organisations it hopes to change. Examples of how cooperation can benefit activists can be found at their Web site www.edf.org.

THE AIM OF TWO-WAY SYMMETRICAL COMMUNICATIONS

Two-way symmetrical communications is proactive. It is based on negotiation and conflict resolution as opposed to defensive communications, which tend to result in conflict. The main focus of negotiation and relationship building is to move both sides slowly and patiently towards a situation that satisfies both parties – a win–win situation, a common ground.

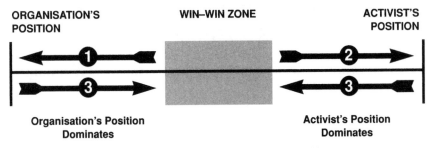

1. Persuasive communication used to dominate activists.
2. Persuasive communication used to dominate organisation.
3. Two-way symmetrical communication used to move both sides to 'win–win' zone.

Figure 3.1 *Two-way symmetry aims to move both sides to a win–win situation*[5]

---

[5] Adapted from Dozier's 'new model of two-way practices' in Dozier, D M *et al* (1995) *Manager's Guide to Excellence in Public Relations and Communications Management*, Lawrence Erlbaum Associates, New Jersey

In Figure 3.1, activists and those they target hold separate and conflicting interests. However, through negotiation and compromise, both sides can find a common ground or win–win zone. In Figure 3.1, the central area depicts the win–win zone. On either side of this zone lies an exploitative situation. To the left of the zone, the organisation tries to dominate activists using powers of persuasion. To the right, activists try to dominate the organisation again through persuasion. These are unstable and unsatisfactory situations where one side wins at the expense of the other – a zero-sum game. In these situations one side will always be unhappy. This is not a good foundation for a solid relationship or a long-term solution.

Compromise on both sides is usually needed to achieve win–win. For example, an organisation may commit itself to improving performance, while activists may relax their demands. Through negotiation both sides work together to move the process forward towards a positive-sum game where all parties are satisfied with compromises made and an atmosphere of openness exists. Moving towards a win–win situation takes time and can only happen in a background of ongoing relationship building, negotiation and conflict resolution using two-way symmetrical communications.

ELEMENTS OF TWO-WAY SYMMETRICAL PROGRAMMES

There are various elements to a two-way symmetrical communications programme.

Research

To facilitate early identification of potential threats, an organisation needs to employ an active programme of research. This allows for a timely and proactive plan of action to help prevent or deal with activism. Without research, an organisation may find itself totally unprepared for activist attack. Chapter 5 outlines the type of research required and how to go about it.

Planning and evaluation

Armed with knowledge acquired from research, a strategic two-way symmetrical communications plan should be developed outlining the goals that need to be achieved. This gives direction and focus to organisational response. Evaluating the effectiveness of the programme on an ongoing basis is also essential to keep it focused, relevant and responsive. How to plan and evaluate two-way symmetrical communications programmes is outlined in Chapter 12.

Relationship building

A key part of the two-way symmetrical communications programme is seeking to develop mutually dependent and lasting relationships with activists and potential activists. Building long-term relationships with groups involves proactive, ongoing, open, two-way dialogue involving regular personal contact and accessibility with all relevant groups regardless of their size. Management must be responsive to what it learns and open to compromise. A step-by-step guide to relationship building, negotiation and conflict resolution is provided in Chapter 6.

Allocating responsibility to relevant staff

The effectiveness of a two-way symmetrical communications programme is contingent on allocating responsibility to staff involved in organisational decision making with the necessary background and education.[6] It is also crucial that management supports the two-way symmetrical approach. These issues are discussed in more detail in Chapter 4.

CASE STUDY: THE LIMITATIONS OF PERSUASION AND THE BENEFITS OF DIALOGUE

A case study carried out by Deborah Anderson in 1992[7] is a good

---

[6] Grunig, L (1992) 'Activism: How it limits the effectiveness of organizations and how excellent public relations departments respond', in J E Grunig (ed), *Excellence in Public Relations and Communication Management*, Lawrence Erlbaum Associates, New Jersey

[7] Anderson, D S (1992) 'Identifying and Responding to Activist Publics: A case study', *Journal of Public Relations Research*, **4** (3), pp 151–65, Lawrence Erlbaum Associates, New Jersey

example of the limited effectiveness of persuasion-based approaches and the improved success of the two-way symmetrical approach when used.

In 1985, a multinational fruit juice manufacturer with headquarters in the United States agreed to acquire 196,000 acres of land in Belize, Central America, 25,000 acres of which were to be set aside for a citrus plantation and an orange juice manufacturing plant. The Belizean government, anxious to encourage foreign investment, encouraged the company to publicise its plans. The company, believing that the news would be positively received, did not envisage any objection and did not conduct research to monitor people's views.

The first sign of activist opposition came a few months after the public announcement of the investment when letters began to arrive from the UK complaining that the company was planning to destroy rainforests in order to plant citrus groves. While the letter-writers were largely misinformed about the company's plans, personnel were shocked into realising that concern for rainforests had become an issue – one that concerned their organisation.

The public relations director, believing that correcting misunderstandings would allay fears, replied in writing. While she did ask people where they had received their information (and learnt that environmental newsletters were the main source), no further steps were taken to investigate the issue. Letters began arriving from other European countries and the company continued to respond in writing. Enquiries revealed that Friends of the Earth (FoE) was a major source of information for objectors. The public relations director telephoned FoE to 'give them the facts'; however she felt that they thought she was being evasive because she could not confirm the company's plans (as the company itself had not finalised them internally).

A local group, the Belize Audubon Society (BAS), began to show its concern. The company set up a meeting with BAS, the outcome of which it viewed as positive. However, it did not maintain an ongoing relationship with this group and later came to regret this as FoE contacted BAS in 1986. When they discovered that the local group was as much in the dark as to the company's plans as they were, FoE went public. They issued a news release to the public and environmental press calling for a worldwide boycott of the company on the basis that it was planning to destroy thousands of acres of rainforest, refusing to do an environmental impact study, deliberately misleading the public and misleading people about its relationship with BAS. Protests took place in Germany and Sweden and environmentalists across Europe became involved, highlighting the issue in their environmental newsletters. Letters of protest poured in.

Up until this point the company had tried to use persuasion to deal with concerns, failing to get involved in dialogue. The first time it used two-way symmetrical communications was more by accident than design. The BBC invited the company to debate the issue with FoE on a worldwide radio broadcast. This was the first face-to-face meeting between both sides and the company's public relations director has since identified it as a turning point in the issue.

When she announced on radio that the company would not go ahead with the project without an environmental impact study, she realised that this had been a major concern for activists. Then, when both sides met privately following the radio interview, she discovered that the activists had escalated the campaign by going public because they felt the organisation was not being responsive to their concerns. After this dialogue, the volume of letters from Europe declined.

Then letters from the United States began to arrive and the company traced these to San Francisco-based environmentalists Rainforest Action Network (RAN). Initially the company tried to persuade this group by sending information. This resulted in a demonstration and picketing. The company then employed two-way communication, inviting the leader of RAN to Belize to examine the proposed project in person. Afterwards, the group discontinued its campaign against the company.

By spring 1987 the protests had subsided when the company decided not to proceed with its development plans in Belize, citing the reasons as the economics of the project, the inability to obtain political risk insurance and an improvement in the US orange market. A meeting was planned to announce the cancellation of the project. About 25 different environmental groups attended. The company's public relations director explained the benefits of this two-way symmetrical meeting:

> This meeting was helpful and insightful for us. We told them our story, and then we asked them what they wanted to say, and we listened. We got raked over the coals, but we learned a lot about the different groups, about the focus of each group and how they operate. Even though they still thought we were in the wrong on the Belize issue, many of them thanked us for having the meeting and told us we were the first company to show that kind of concern.

In 1988, in partnership with the Belize Audubon Society and the Massachusetts Audubon Society, the company established a national park and a conservation programme to which it donated 42,000 acres and US $50,000. The public relations director continued to keep in contact with the groups she had met, subscribe to international environmental newsletters, attend environmental conferences and make regular personal contacts with activists to keep them informed.

What can be learnt from this experience?

- A programme of research is crucial to identify threats.
- There is a need to communicate with relevant audiences before a plan is announced.
- Activists are very effective at communicating with one another, making them a global threat. In this case, an issue relating to an area of rainforest in South America met with objection in the UK, continental Europe and the United States.
- If organisations fail to listen to activists, they fail to realise that they may in fact be able to meet their concerns (the company had planned an environmental impact study well before it was announced, failing to realise its importance to FoE).
- Persuasion-based, non-listening communications can worsen the situation.
- Once concerns are identified the company can work towards addressing them.
- Two-way symmetrical communications offer a way forward where the company does not have to give in to activists or persuade them to give in.
- Failure to build and maintain ongoing two-way relationships with groups (eg BAS) may mean that the organisation risks losing an ally that could help the organisation in dealing with other activists.
- It is never too late to move to two-way communications.
- Ongoing two-way symmetrical communications help organisations keep in touch with the views of a key audience.
- Dealing with activists through two-way symmetrical communications can improve performance.

SUMMARY

- The views of activists and organisations are not as disparate as either side would believe. However, a lack of trust keeps both sides apart.
- Activists are less likely to be aggressive or seek third-party

involvement if the targeted organisation takes a cooperative stance.

- Two-way symmetrical communications, based on proactive negotiation and conflict resolution, offers a way forward in dealing with activists.
- Employing two-way symmetrical communications means that the organisation seeks to understand and work with activists towards a situation that benefits both sides. Compromise on both sides is likely to be needed.
- Emphasis is on building lasting relationships with activists and responding and adjusting to their changing views.
- Research into the organisation's changing environment and the development of a strategic communications plan are key elements of two-way symmetrical communications. Ongoing evaluation helps to keep the plan effective and relevant.

4

Appointing responsibility for activism in-house

Allocating responsibility for activism to a member of staff with suitable background and experience is a key part of two-way symmetrical communications and one of the first steps in tackling activism. This chapter advises on how to select a suitable candidate and build on his or her skills. It also highlights the need for management to support and be committed to the concept of two-way symmetrical communications.

WHO TO CHOOSE

Ideally, the person allocated responsibility for activism should be a manager, with good communication skills and in-depth knowledge of the organisation.

A manager

He or she should be a member of and have credibility with the management team in order to be able to impart bad news and recommend brave measures without fear of reproach. It is a waste to allocate resources to activism if the person responsible is afraid to speak honestly and openly with the dominant coalition (organisational decision-makers) about what needs to be done.

A communicator

Because two-way symmetrical communications are based on negotiation and conflict resolution, the person with overall responsibility should have excellent communication skills, ideally with a background and experience in this area. The following are particularly relevant: public relations, communications, human resources, psychology, corporate affairs, etc. The candidate must understand and be committed to two-way symmetrical communications as the way forward in dealing with activists.

Knowledgeable about the business

The person with responsibility for activism needs to have a good understanding of the organisation and line of business it operates in as activists can raise many issues. These need to be addressed with ability and confidence. Additionally, knowledge of key legislation and regulations affecting the business is needed for the individual to anticipate and prepare for any changes that may need to be made to the business. An organisation that does not keep up to date with (or ahead of) legislative or regulatory requirements puts itself at risk of activist pressure.

TRAINING

The person with overall responsibility for activists needs to understand and be able to conduct two-way symmetrical communications programmes. This requires the following skills:

- the ability to coordinate a research programme;
- the ability to develop a strategic communications plan;

- fine-tuned negotiation and conflict resolution skills;
- an understanding of risk communications, community relations, media relations and crisis management.

These skills can be easily acquired through basic training in any of the areas the individual is unfamiliar with. In addition to developing new skills, it is also good practice to build on existing skills through ongoing training. Although this may involve investing resources, it helps to build confidence, morale and job satisfaction in addition to equipping staff better to handle threats.

THE BENEFITS OF CAREFUL SELECTION AND TRAINING

Well-trained communicators with the ear of organisational decision-makers perform better as they have greater influence and are given freer rein to implement two-way symmetrical programmes. In fact, research shows that the more educated and experienced a communicator, the more likely he or she is to be represented in the dominant coalition.[1]

MANAGEMENT MUST SUPPORT TWO-WAY SYMMETRICAL COMMUNICATIONS

While careful selection and training of the candidate are crucial, equally important is a commitment by organisational decision-makers to the concept of two-way symmetrical communications.[2] Management needs to understand and expect two-way communication in order for it to be seen as essential. Should members of management be unfamiliar with or unconvinced by the two-way symmetrical process, communicators need to educate them of the benefits. Case histories and books such as this may prove useful in this regard.

---

[1] Pollack, R A (1986) *Testing the Grunig Organizational Theory in Scientific Organizations: Public relations and the values of the dominant coalition*, Master's thesis, University of Maryland, College Park

[2] Grunig, L (1992) 'Activism: How it limits the effectiveness of organizations and how excellent public relations departments respond', in J E Grunig (ed) *Excellence in Public Relations and Communication Management*, Lawrence Erlbaum Associates, New Jersey

BUILDING A TEAM

While overall responsibility for activists should rest with one person to ensure that the programme is well managed and clear messages are presented to decision-makers, there should also be a team of support staff involved. One of the most important reasons for this is to create a chain of referral in the event of a surprise activist attack on the organisation. If the key manager is not present, there will be others who can be called upon in a particular order who will be familiar with the situation.

On a day-to-day basis, a support team is also useful in terms of job delegation, stimulating ideas, keeping motivated, etc. When choosing a team, it is useful to select people with a variety of communication skills such as research, report writing, media relations and community relations. Participation of staff in such ongoing problem solving can help to increase teamwork, morale and job satisfaction.

DEVELOPMENT OF THE INDIVIDUAL

Dealing with activists can provide an opportunity for individuals to highlight their role within the organisation. For example, those who become involved in organisation-activist committees are likely to be regarded as responsible for creating a 'win–win situation', enhancing management's perception of them and improving their career options.[3] The converse is also true, in that if the communicator does not become involved in two-way communications it is likely that management will revert to traditional, ineffective defence mechanisms when responding to activists.[4]

---

[3] Grunig, L (1992) 'Activism: How it limits the effectiveness of organizations and how excellent public relations departments respond', in J E Grunig (ed) *Excellence in Public Relations and Communication Management*, Lawrence Erlbaum Associates, New Jersey
[4] Jones, B L and Chase, W H (1979) 'Managing public policy issues', *Public Relations Review*, **5**, pp 3–23

ARE ORGANISATIONS PREPARED FOR ACTIVIST PRESSURE?: RESEARCH

Larissa Grunig's five-year research of 34 case studies of organisational behaviour during conflict with activist groups[5] revealed that only five of the 34 people interviewed who had responsibility for dealing with activists had formal training in public relations. Very few of those responsible for activists employed two-way symmetrical communications. In general, lack of research skills was regarded as the greatest deficiency and this lessened the communicators' ability to monitor issues and the public, leading to situations where many were caught off guard.

Interestingly, Grunig found that small to medium-sized companies performed better as they felt more threatened and tended to consult experts such as public relations and legal professionals. Moderate-sized companies relied on in-house public relations departments while large organisations tended to cling to established public relations programmes, ignoring the concerns of groups – those that recognised the threat tended to call on their industry association rather than outside experts for help.

In a study of seven pharmaceutical and chemical manufacturers operating in Cork Harbour, Ireland,[6] it was found that the only company that had developed relations with single-issue environmentalists had allocated responsibility to an individual with a communications and psychology background with well-practised negotiation skills. Importantly, the managing director had been fully behind the approach and very involved in negotiations. This was the only company researched that employed two-way symmetrical communications with single-issue environmental groups. Significantly, the environmental group involved spoke highly of the company saying that it would find it difficult to criticise it.

---

[5] Grunig, L (1992) 'Activism: How it limits the effectiveness of organizations and how excellent public relations departments respond', in J E Grunig (ed) *Excellence in Public Relations and Communication Management*, Lawrence Erlbaum Associates, New Jersey
[6] Deegan, D (1999) *An Examination of How Pharmaceutical and Chemical Manufacturers Located in Cork Harbour Relate to Environmental Activist Groups, December 1998–February 1999*, Master's thesis, Dublin Institute of Technology

SUMMARY

- Allocating responsibility for activism to a person with suitable background and experience is a key part of two-way symmetrical communications.
- Equally crucial is management's support of the two-way symmetrical process.
- The main criteria are that the person is:
  - a manager who has the ear of the dominant coalition;
  - a communicator, committed to two-way symmetrical communications;
  - knowledgeable of the organisation, business and relevant legislation.
- Key skills required, which can be learnt, include:
  - research skills;
  - the ability to develop a communications programme;
  - negotiation and conflict resolution skills;
  - knowledge of risk communications, community relations, media relations and crisis management.
- A support team should be appointed to facilitate delegation of tasks and to ensure that there is a chain of referral in the event of an emergency.
- Proactive management of activist pressure provides an opportunity to highlight the importance of one's role within the organisation.
- Research shows that there is a direct relationship between the level of education and background of communicators, and their performance in dealing with activists.

5

Get to know 'the enemy'

Ongoing research is essential to enable organisations to prepare for and to adapt to changes in their environment such as the advent of activist groups that may prove a threat. Without undertaking research, organisations may find themselves totally unprepared for activist attack. This chapter identifies the type of research that organisations need to undertake to help equip them to deal with activists.

WHAT TO RESEARCH

Research is an intrinsic part of two-way symmetrical programmes in helping to keep an organisation in tune with its environment, sensitive to any changes that may occur. Studies reveal that the level of research carried out by communicators is an indicator of excellence.[1] The following areas should be researched:

---

[1] Dozier D M *et al* (1995) *Managers' Guide to Excellence in Public Relations and Communication Management*, Lawrence Erlbaum Associates, New Jersey

- all the possible activist groups that may prove a threat;
- the goals of these activists;
- their views of the organisation;
- public opinion of the organisation, including identifying potential threats;
- organisational performance in potentially contentious areas, eg the environment;
- outside influences such as political movements, legislation, technological developments, etc.

Identifying activists that may prove a threat

In order to identify groups that may threaten an organisation, it is necessary to carry out an issues audit, in other words, an examination of the organisation itself for any potentially contentious areas. To be objective and thorough, management should wear an activist's hat or ideally hire an outside consultant to apply what Greenpeace refers to as 'the salami principle', that is, mentally slicing the organisation into small pieces to identify vulnerable areas.[2] Asking the following kinds of questions should help to identify which type/s of groups may prove a threat:

- Do any of the organisation's activities have a negative impact, for example, on the environment, animal rights, workers' rights, etc?
- Could any of the processes carried out be deemed hazardous?
- Might any of the products be considered harmful in any way?
- Are there any areas where the organisation might be considered to be behaving unethically?

Once the types of groups have been identified, the next step is to make a list of all of the actual groups in existence that slot into these categories. This should include large, international groups as well as smaller local ones, not forgetting local residents' associations which can prove powerful activists as they are often those with most to lose because of their proximity to a manufacturing plant, for example.

---

[2] Duncan, C (1996) 'How to Manage an International PR Issue', *IPR Journal*, January, IPR, London

In identifying activists, the following methods can prove useful:

- *Brainstorming* with a group of staff members can help to build an exhaustive list of groups. Brainstorming can be particularly useful in pinpointing local groups.
- *The Internet* is a useful source of information in highlighting activist groups, both local and international. In addition to traditional search methods, there is a Web site named Norbert's Bookmarks (www.dfg-vk.de/english/mission.htm) that provides an extensive database of activists worldwide under a wide range of headings such as human rights, environment, Third World, disarmament, etc. Many activist Web sites have 'links' to other relevant sites so, for example, by visiting the Greenpeace site (www.greenpeace.org), one can access a list of other relevant activist sites that can be visited. Therefore, as research progresses, more and more avenues open up. Visiting activist Web sites may also be useful in terms of trying to ascertain if the organisation may be a potential target. Friends of the Earth's UK site (www.foe.co.uk), for example, features 'Factory Watch', providing data on factories causing pollution in England, Wales, Scotland and Northern Ireland. Relevant organisations should know whether or not they are on this list.
- *Media searches* of trade publications and general media can also prove useful in highlighting relevant activist groups. News clipping services can be employed to carry out retrospective media searches as well as ongoing media monitoring.
- *Trade bodies and industry contacts* can also provide useful information based on their own experiences and knowledge of groups.

Following an exhaustive search, a list of all the groups with potential to threaten the organisation should be drawn up. Responsibility for regular updating of this list should be allocated to a relevant member of staff. Ongoing research should be instigated and the list kept up to date.

Identifying activist goals

The next stage in the research process is to investigate the goals of each of the groups that have been identified. It is important to learn as much as possible about each group such as the key players, their views and how decisions are made. For example, is decision making centralised or decentralised? Is there one key individual responsible for decision making or is the process more democratic?

Once again, the Internet can prove a valuable tool in this regard. Many groups, particularly environmentalists, have Web sites containing information such as a background on the group, details of their current and past campaigns, latest press releases, editions of their newsletter (if they produce one), etc. Most will have an interaction facility that can be used to request further information.

Media searches can prove useful in identifying the type of tactics used by groups and the main issues and organisations they target. Media reports on issues relating to the organisation may be a sign that it will be targeted. For example,[3] people in the UK began to object to mobile phone masts following a much reported legal case in the United States involving a man who alleged that he developed a brain tumour from electromagnetic radiation from his mobile phone. Mobile phone masts had been installed for about two years in the UK without objection prior to this. The case drew media and public attention to the possible dangers associated with mobile phones and their masts. Since then people have been objecting to masts in the UK.[4]

Reports of new research can also act as early warning signals that an organisation may be targeted. Particular attention should be paid to specialist media such as environmental publications as they are likely to be first to publish such research.

Methods of searching the media include visiting media Web sites, scanning back copies of newspapers through microfiche and checking library files under the activist group's name. Alternatively, a press clippings firm can be hired. They are inexpensive and can save valuable time. Many activists produce publications such as newsletters that can also provide useful background information.

Because groups tend to mistrust organisations, it is not advisable at the initial stages of research to contact groups directly to request information as it may draw attention to the organisation

---

[3] Interview (20 April 2000) with Nick Sharples, Community Relations Manager, One 2 One
[4] *Ibid.*

before it is ready to respond. If e-mailing or requesting information from a Web site, it is best not to use the organisation's address. Later, once contact has been made with the group, ongoing relationship building will help to keep the organisation updated on its goals and views.

Having identified the goals of the relevant activist groups, management should work through the implications to the organisation should each of these goals be achieved, so that plans can be made to deal with all eventualities.

If an organisation is suspicious of the motivations of a group, it should investigate how it receives its funding. As outlined in Chapter 1, 'front groups' can be established to damage an organisation's competitiveness. When Browning-Ferris Industries (BFI) were surprised by 'a highly sophisticated seismic critique' submitted to the authorities by a neighbourhood group, 'The North Valley Coalition of Concerned Citizens', it carried out its own investigation into the group's funding. It discovered that BFI's main competitor, WMX Technologies, had funded the study.[5]

How activists view the organisation

Searching the Internet, media and publications produced by activists to identify activist goals may also reveal how activists view the organisation. However, until both sides actually sit down together it is often difficult to assess true views and their accuracy. Once both sides do begin to work together, however, there is a model that can be used to clarify each side's views of the other. Known as the 'co-orientational' model, it is discussed in Chapter 12 as it is primarily used to evaluate the effectiveness of two-way symmetrical programmes in bringing both sides closer together.

Public opinion and potential threats

Studying the opinions people have of the organisation should help to detect views that may become a threat, affording the opportunity to act early to restore public confidence. Market research agencies can be hired to conduct what is called 'primary research', ie private, original research specifically conducted for the

---

[5] Denzenhall, E (1999) *Nail 'Em: Confronting high-profile attacks on celebrities & business,* Prometheus Books, New York

organisation (as distinct from secondary research or desk research which monitors existing work, eg the media, Internet, published material, etc).

What do you research?

Primary research can serve two purposes. It can monitor people's attitudes, how they are changing and for whom they are changing. It can also detect existing or potential threats, for example, people who may become activists. Typical issues to be investigated include the importance and relevance to people of general issues such as the environment as well as the opinion of the organisation under various headings such as:

● general opinion of the organisation;
● anything the organisation does well;
● any concerns about the organisation;
● the degree of knowledge on the organisation;
● views of the organisation under specified relevant categories such as:
    – its products;
    – its impact on the environment;
    – its treatment of staff;
    – its manufacturing process;
    – its marketing, promotional, packaging, distribution.

Who do you research?

The population to be researched will depend on the type of organisation involved, the type of information sought, the localisation of an issue and the budget available. Ultimately, the population to be studied is at the discretion of the organisation and may take in the entire population of the country, or may focus more specifically on a region or demographic group.

Employees, customers and suppliers are closest to the organisation and generally know it better than the public at large. Identifying the concerns of these groups is not only useful in terms of addressing them but may also act as an early warning mechanism for issues that may ultimately concern the public. Because of their closeness to the organisation, interviewees need to be reassured of confidentiality.

As surveys are time-consuming and expensive, they may be

conducted as part of an overall management review for improving organisational performance generally.

How do you research?

The type of research carried out will depend on a number of factors:

- who is being researched, eg the general public, employees, etc;
- the type of information required;
- the budget available.

There are two broad categories of research that can be used, quantitative and qualitative:

- Quantitative research involves *measuring* who, how many, attitudes, image, etc so that an identifiable numerical definition can be accorded to any given situation, for example, 80 per cent of the population are 'concerned about the environment'. Quantitative research typically involves obtaining information from a sample that is representative of the target population. If surveys are repeated, quantitative research helps to identify trends and changes in public opinion, eg an increase in the percentage of people concerned for the environment.
- Qualitative research seeks to *understand* rather than to measure and investigates the why behind people's actions and emotions. It is a more in-depth approach involving much smaller sample sizes than quantitative research.

Both types of research can be employed together as one complements the other.

Quantitative research

Quantitative research involves the selection of a sample of a population for interview and the use of a structured questionnaire to source the required information. The sample selected should ideally be representative of the population being investigated, eg have the same demography, behavioural characteristics, etc.

An example of the type of information one can investigate can be seen from research carried out by United Utilities, a group of businesses providing essential services including water and wastewater services, electricity distribution and telecommunications to people all over the world. By looking at the table of results (Figure 5.1), one can see the type of information sought. One can also see how simplicity in presenting results can give a clear picture of how an organisation is viewed at any given time. By repeating the same survey, for example following a communications programme (or alternatively an incident), the impact on the organisation's reputation can be gauged.

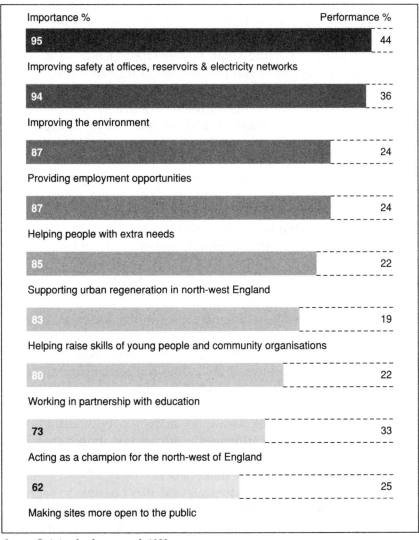

Source: Opinion leader research 1999

Figure 5.1 *Stakeholder views on United Utilities' priorities and performance*

Interviews can be conducted in different ways, for example face-to-face in a person's home, on the street, by telephone, post or self-completion. The method used will depend largely on the population being researched and the issues being investigated. There are pros and cons for the different methods.

Face-to-face interviews in respondents' homes are ideal for long interviews and facilitate the showing of stimulus material; but these studies are expensive. Face-to-face interviews on the street are less expensive, but are only suited to short surveys and where geography plays an important role. Telephone interviewing is ideal for studies involving small key groups, such as employees, customers and suppliers that can be easily targeted through databases, but the interview needs to be short and stimulus material cannot be shown. Self-completion surveys are very economical, but the sample is self-selecting and response rates are typically low.

When developing a questionnaire, it is important to keep in mind that questions should be carefully worded to avoid ambiguity, misunderstandings or leading those being interviewed. While this is the market research agency's area of expertise, it is nonetheless advisable to check wording when finalising the questionnaire to facilitate useful interpretation of final results.

Identifying the public likely to become activists

One of the benefits of quantitative research is that in investigating opinions it is possible to identify the public likely to become activists. This can be done by adapting Grunig's situational theory.[6] This identifies three types of public, namely, latent, aware and active. The latent public does not recognise a situation as problematic. When it recognises the problem it becomes aware. It becomes active when it organises to do something about the problem. To move from aware to active, people need to be convinced that they can influence the situation – should they hold any preconceived attitudes preventing them becoming active they will need information to alter these beliefs.

When conducting quantitative surveys it is possible to segment the population at each stage. Members of the public in the active category are, needless to say, those most likely to become activists.

---

[6] Grunig's situational theory has been well summarised by Pavlik, J N (1987) *Public Relations: What research tells us*, Sage Publications, Newbury Park, California

A breakdown can be provided of the different types of people in this group, for example, male/female, age, class, what media they read/watch/listen to, etc. This information should prove very useful when targeting these groups for communication.

Limitations to quantitative research

The style of a quantitative interview, regardless of approach, means that there is a limit to the level of 'in-depthness' to which issues can be investigated. Questions are fixed and the structure rigid. Should greater understanding be required there is a role for qualitative research.

Qualitative research

Qualitative research involves sourcing in-depth information as to why people hold certain views. It may be used to investigate issues or concerns identified in quantitative research. It can also be a very useful tool at the start of a research programme if an organisation is unsure what direction to take. In this case qualitative research helps to identify the main issues causing people concern. This helps to ensure that any subsequent quantitative research investigates issues of relevance.

Focus groups are the most common method of qualitative research and involve stimulating detailed discussion among a small group (approximately six to eight) of a chosen audience, with a group moderator guiding the discussion rather than questioning the group. For example, in order to try to understand the attitudes held toward genetically modified foods, the moderator would tease out:

- the group's attitudes to food in general;
- what they are looking for in a food;
- why certain food types are bought and not others;
- how food is bought;
- whether or not ingredients are checked;
- what GM foods are;
- what is wrong/right with GM foods;
- whether they buy GM foods, knowingly/unwittingly;
- why they do not buy GM foods;
- where they think their concerns originated.

The key to understanding motivations, emotions, etc is not just listening to what people are saying, but also how they say it, body language, group dynamics and reactions to stimulus material.

As an alternative to groups, in-depth, one-to-one interviews may also be carried out. As these are expensive and time-consuming they are usually restricted to key audiences that are difficult to reach, eg opinion leaders, the medical profession, solicitors, etc. The qualitative process remains the same.

The simplest and most effective way to carry out qualitative research is to employ a market research agency specialising in investigating motivations.

How one company uses research

The United Utilities (UU) group of businesses carries out regular research to gauge the opinion of customers, stakeholders and employees as to their level of satisfaction with company performance. In 1998, UU completed a two-year strategic review of its impact on society, researching stakeholders' expectations and the company's level of understanding of these and seeking to gauge best practice. This involved a sample of over 500 interviewees including national and regional politicians and pressure groups, consumer groups, customers, employees and business partners. The results of this research are then used in the formation of two-way symmetrical communication programmes where the views of stakeholders are taken into consideration. Subsequent research has been useful in reinforcing results.

Secondary research

Secondary research, involving the monitoring of existing material, can also be employed to investigate opinion. Views expressed in the media, on the Internet, in publications, etc can be gauged. For example, opinions expressed in the media can both reflect and influence public opinion. Letters to the editor are of particular interest in identifying issues of common concern at any given time. Ongoing media monitoring can be employed for mentions of the organisation or of relevant general issues (eg environmental issues).

Encouraging feedback

Another effective, proactive and ongoing method of gauging

people's views and identifying potential threats is to be open about the organisation's activities and to actively encourage feedback. Shell UK, for example, following the Brent Spar incident, learnt that they had underestimated the level of public interest in their activities. Now, in an effort to keep abreast of views and issues, the company talks more about what it does and actively seeks feedback, for example through its Web site (www.shell.co.uk). This allows the company an opportunity to identify issues, enter into early dialogue with those concerned and seek to address the cause of concerns.

In one of its first moves towards more open communication with the public, in the wake of Brent Spar in 1996, Shell UK published a detailed environmental report that encouraged members of the public to offer feedback. They then held a 'Dialogue Event' in 1997 where representatives of interest groups, regulatory bodies, industry and others were invited to discuss issues of concern in an open forum.[7] The event pinpointed a wide range of environmental issues that needed to be addressed as well as the need for increased openness and transparency in decision making. Each year, Shell UK now conducts a MORI poll of 'Corporate Social Responsibility' and publishes a *Report to Society*, that seeks to address issues of concern in detail.

Organisational performance

The organisation itself should be studied in terms of its performance in areas that might be targeted by activists. For example, a chemical manufacturer will need to study:

- production procedures;
- disposal of waste;
- adherence to legislation;
- monitoring procedures;
- the degree of and type of complaints received;
- employee awareness of environmental procedures;
- employee satisfaction;
- adequacy of financial and human resources in vulnerable areas.

---

[7] Shell UK (1998) *Report To Society*, Shell UK Ltd, London

Shell UK, through its 1997 MORI poll on corporate social responsibility, learnt the importance of the following areas to the public:[8]

- how it looks after its employees;
- how it protects the local environment;
- how it reduces pollution;
- how it helps job creation;
- how it becomes involved in local events;
- how open it is and how it keeps the public informed.

Areas that need to be improved should be improved. However, the fact that an organisation meets the requirements of legislation does not make it immune to activist pressure, as Shell found out when it tried to dispose of Brent Spar.

Outside influences

An organisation should keep up to date on any outside influences that may affect its functioning. These include pending legislation, political movements, technological developments, environmental initiatives, etc. Legislation that is to come into effect in five years time may take that amount of time to prepare for in terms of changes that may be needed to corporate procedure, such as sourcing alternative materials or processes. Failure to plan ahead to keep in line with new regulations, work practices, views, etc leaves one open to activist attack.

One of the simplest ways to keep abreast of relevant initiatives is through industry groups and trade bodies, whose function it is to provide this information. Also to be recommended are ongoing reviews of publications such as trade journals which print topical articles before they reach the mainstream media.

CASE STUDY: THE TIN CAN INDUSTRY SEES THE NEED TO CHANGE

In the 1970s the tin can industry in the UK learnt of new research into possible health risks associated with lead, which was being used in the manufacture of cans. This was preliminary research and there was no regulation on the issue. However, the industry realised the possible

---

[8] Shell UK (1998) *Report to Society*, Shell UK Ltd, London

future implications for its business should expert and public opinion turn against lead. It informed government of the research and steps it planned to take to remove lead from tin cans both in the short and long term.

Removing lead from the manufacturing process would be a long and expensive process. In the short term, the industry focused its efforts on those most at risk, babies (as their brains were still developing and some babies had a very high canned food proportion in their total diet and relatively higher lead exposure). Lead solder was replaced with pure tin at considerable cost.

At the same time, the industry embarked on a multi-million pound conversion of adult food cans, accelerating the introduction of two lead-free technologies.

By the early 1980s these conversions were well underway when the issue of the dangers of lead exploded into public awareness. A major, high profile campaign against lead in petrol, the Clear campaign, was launched in the UK. Had the tin can industry not taken action when it learnt of the potential dangers of lead, the spotlight could have swung aggressively in its direction. As it happened, industry representatives approached the campaigners to discuss the issue and the work that was being carried out in removing lead from tin cans. Clear agreed to avoid focusing on tin cans and to keep their focus on petrol. The changeover process proceeded unhindered and was complete by the mid-to-late 1980s.

RESEARCH CRITERIA

A programme of research should be developed involving all or a combination of the above types of research. The programme should then be instigated in a planned and methodical manner. Results from one type of research (eg quantitative surveys) will influence other types (eg the focus of qualitative research); therefore the programme will need to have a degree of flexibility built in at the outset. It goes without saying that research should be ongoing and initiated before a group threatens the organisation. All information gleaned from research should be documented and updated regularly so the organisation is up to speed on the environment it works in, ready to implement any changes needed at the earliest opportunity.

SUMMARY

- Without research, an organisation may find itself totally unprepared for activist attack.
- Research should include:
  - all the possible activist groups that may threaten the organisation, their goals and views of the organisation;
  - the public likely to become activists;
  - public opinion of the organisation;
  - organisational performance;
  - outside influences such as political, legislative and technological developments.
- Research tools include the Internet; media searches; industry groups and trade bodies, primary research (quantitative and qualitative surveys of the public, employees, customers and suppliers, etc).
- Research should be ongoing and initiated before a group threatens the organisation. All information gleaned from research should be documented and updated regularly.

6

Relationship building, negotiation and conflict resolution

A proactive strategy of relationship building, negotiation and conflict resolution is a cornerstone of this book's recommended approach to dealing with activists. This chapter guides the reader through the various stages involved, including which groups to approach, when to approach them and in what order, how to make contact, how to keep the lines of communication open and how to progress the relationship towards a win–win solution.

WHICH GROUPS TO APPROACH

Ideally, all groups, regardless of size, should be approached. There may be a temptation to ignore smaller groups, arguing that their size does not warrant expenditure of resources. This temptation should be dismissed as, ironically, it is the smaller groups that tend to be most efficient in pressuring organisations because they are more likely to be committed, motivated and active.[1,2]

Hostile groups with entrenched beliefs can be approached; however, special precautions are needed. This issue is addressed specifically in Chapter 7.

WHEN TO APPROACH

The ideal time to approach activists or potential activists is as soon as they have been identified as a threat. Ideally, groups should be approached *before* they have formed opinions specifically on the organisation. If activists' minds are already set against an organisation, negotiation will be more difficult. For example, groups are less likely to want to negotiate if they have already committed to a public campaign against the organisation that they have invested time and money researching. If they have highlighted this campaign in the media they may fear that negotiation with their targets will be viewed as a U-turn in their approach or an admission that their accusations were wrong. Negotiation, activists may feel, also risks taking the momentum out of a potentially successful strategy. The solution is to talk early.

If an organisation is planning an activity that it thinks might meet with objection, for example, locating a new refuse dump for municipal waste, it is advisable to consult all relevant groups well in advance of seeking planning permission. Involving potential objectors in the decision-making process at its earliest stage can increase the chances that they will accept final decisions more easily. The case history in Chapter 9 relating to Lothian Regional Council highlights this point.

---

[1] Grunig, L (1992) 'Activism: How it limits the effectiveness of organizations and how excellent public relations departments respond', in J E Grunig (ed) *Excellence in Public Relations and Communication Management*, Lawrence Erlbaum Associates, New Jersey
[2] Olson, M (1982) *The Logic of Collective Action: Public goods and the theory of groups*, Harvard University Press, Cambridge, MA

WHO TO APPROACH FIRST

Should research identify more than one activist group as a potential threat, as is usually the case, the organisation needs to make a decision as to which group to approach first. Research plays a crucial role in learning about the different groups so that a strategy can be developed, outlining the order in which they might be approached.

Less hostile groups

Approaching 'the enemy' can seem daunting and for many will go against the grain. There is an advantage, therefore, in working with a less hostile group first. Initial mistakes are more likely to be forgiven and an understanding of activists and the way they think can be more easily developed. Confidence can be built and negotiation skills fine-tuned.

Because they have a common interest, special interest groups such as environmentalists tend to be knowledgeable about one another. Some may have campaigned together in the past. Building relations with less hostile groups first may lead to valuable information on other activists, particularly the more hostile ones. This can be very useful when deciding when and how to approach such groups.

A less hostile group can on occasion facilitate an introduction to a more antagonistic group. This is advantageous as the initial sting of suspicion may be eased when the hostile group learns of the progress that has already been made by the organisation working with the other group. A reassurance is given that the company is putting its money where its mouth is and its commitments are genuine.

Immediate threats

Groups that are close to targeting the company should be a priority as they are likely to present the greatest threat in the short term. Research will help to identify such groups. If, for example, workers' rights activists are running a campaign targeting abuses in Third World factories, an organisation involved in operating manufacturing plants in Asia should reasonably expect to be targeted, especially if the company has been mentioned at any point, eg in a specialist publication. It is best not to delay if a group seems close to targeting the organisation.

Some organisations are unlucky enough to have activist groups actually set up to target them specifically, eg McDonald's and Nike. Such groups are, of course, a priority.

Local groups

For those involved in manufacturing, emissions or any process that may be seen to affect the health and lifestyles of their neighbours, local residents and their associations make up arguably the most important audience. They are closest to the organisation, have most to fear and as such can prove extremely powerful activists. There should be no delay in seeking to build relations with this crucial audience and, in addition to the general advice offered in this chapter, a special chapter on community relations has been included in this book (Chapter 9).

Some special interest groups such as environmentalists concentrate their activities on one region (eg San Diego Environment Now). These groups are more likely to pose a threat to organisations in their catchment area than large, international groups that are unlikely to target an organisation unless it serves to highlight current campaigns or issues.

THINK LIKE AN ACTIVIST

Once a strategy has been developed as to which groups to approach first, it is important to try to enter the mindset of activists by imagining oneself as an activist. For example, trying to feel and live the mistrust that activists have for organisations should help one to prepare for the initial scepticism that activists feel when organisations approach them to negotiate. Seeing things from the activists' point of view helps to highlight the need to explain intentions clearly, that is, to open the lines of communication and to seek to work together to improve the situation in such a way that is satisfactory to both sides.

Thinking like an activist may go some way to avoiding simple but disastrous mistakes such as sending a letter to environmentalists on expensive, non-recycled glossy paper. These errors can send the following signal: 'This is what they say but this is what they do'.

MAKING INITIAL CONTACT

Because of the scepticism that is likely to exist, an initial introduction through a third party that has a relationship with both sides can be advantageous if it can be arranged. The suggestion of holding discussions can be made in a less formal, more personal way. The third party has the ear of the group to outline the benefits of dialogue. This kind of link-up can be preferable to 'cold calling' the group because to a degree the third party is endorsing the organisation as worth listening to.

Brainstorming can help to identify relevant third parties. The following check list may prove useful:

- employees of the organisation;
- family members of employees;
- friends of employees;
- members of civic organisations;
- non-executive directors (who often have an extensive contact base);
- technical consultants used by the organisation (who may have had previous contact with groups);
- other activist groups with which the organisation has relations.

If no mutual contacts can be identified, the person making the initial contact should be sufficiently high ranking within the organisation, ideally the managing director. This emphasises the commitment by the organisation to negotiation. He or she should aim to communicate directly with the key decision-maker in the group. The aim of initial contact should be to open discussions through an exploratory meeting between key decision-makers on both sides.

Prior to meeting the group, research will have revealed as much as possible about the group, ie the main personnel, key decision-maker/s, main areas of interest, goals, views of the organisation, etc. This information should be reviewed prior to the meeting.

OPENING NEGOTIATIONS

At the outset of the first meeting, the objectives of dialogue should be explained openly. Activist views should be sought and listened to and the temptation to persuade avoided. A concerted effort should be made to try to see the group's fears as legitimate even if they may seem illogical. When questioned about the organisation, answers given should not be too technical and should be easily understood. Depending on the level of progress being made and the level of cooperation being given by the group, it can be useful to suggest the involvement of an independent expert at this stage.

It is important not to expect too much from the initial meeting. If the lines of communication are opened and a subsequent meeting arranged, this is a positive achievement. If the meeting does not go according to plan, the organisation should not abandon efforts. When management at SmithKline Beecham's (SB) plant in Cork, Ireland, approached local group, Cork Environmental Alliance (CEA) to build relations, the group walked out of the first meeting. SB later learnt that the CEA had felt that the company had been trying to blind them with science. SB decided to try again, offering to fund an independent expert to act on behalf of the CEA as a technical expert. The CEA selected an academic at a local university and the process moved forward.[3]

INVOLVING INDEPENDENT THIRD PARTIES

An independent third-party expert brings the benefits of his or her knowledge and experience to the table in advising on approaches toward organisational improvement. If activists put forward unrealistic requests, the independent expert can highlight the fact that they are unrealistic and suggest a workable alternative or compromise. The organisation is not dismissing activist concerns and the relationship between both sides is not compromised.

When selecting a third-party arbitrator, it is crucial to choose an individual who is publicly regarded as neutral, with no

---

[3] Deegan, D (1999) *An Examination of How Pharmaceutical and Chemical Manufacturers located in Cork Harbour Relate to Environmental Activist Groups, December 1998–February 1999*, Master's thesis, Dublin Institute of Technology

favouritism for either side. Ideally, activists should select the individual so that the organisation cannot later be accused of choosing a partisan person. However, both sides must be happy with the person allocated the task. Because activists can have limited funds, it can be a positive gesture for the organisation to offer to fund this individual.

If workable steps are put forward by the third-party expert, the organisation can commit to implementing these over a realistic and agreed upon time period. Compromise is likely to be needed on both sides.

MAINTAINING ONGOING CONTACT WITH ACTIVISTS

Ongoing contact is important to keep the lines of communication open. Regular meetings can be arranged, for example initially every six to eight weeks. The person with responsibility for activists must attend each meeting, with regular appearances by the managing director. Other members of the team responsible for activism can attend meetings; however, care should be taken to avoid overstaffing as this may present an aggressive stance. Members of staff who get on well with activist members should be present at meetings and conversely those who do not should not.

Ongoing meetings require direction – progress needs to be made in order for both sides to consider the expenditure of resources worthwhile. Goals need to be set. Initially, the most important goal is for both sides to develop an understanding of each other. At the first meeting, a situation known as 'wedging' usually exists – each side holds its own view and rejects that of the other, making progress unlikely. The objective of early dialogue is to stimulate 'hedging', a situation where both sides can accept two apparently conflicting views – their own and that of their counterpart. So, for example, environmentalists can retain their concerns for the environment while understanding the obstacles a pharmaceutical manufacturer may face in reaching their demands of zero emissions. The organisation in return can hedge its knowledge of the obstacles it faces against environmentalists' real concern for the environment.

To achieve hedging there must be a joint commitment to work together to go as far as is possible to achieve the desired situation. In the above case, the commitment might be for environmentalists and manufacturer to develop plans jointly to reduce emissions to as close to zero as is possible. Once hedging is achieved, the negotiation process can move forward with both sides seeing benefits in working together.

THE LONG-TERM GOAL OF NEGOTIATION

The long-term goal of ongoing negotiation is to edge both sides carefully towards a mutually beneficial situation. First, both parties should seek to work together to achieve a result that is satisfactory to both – a so-called 'win–win situation'.[4]

To achieve this, both sides are likely to have to compromise – activists by relaxing their expectations or by lengthening their deadlines – organisations by improving their operations as much as possible in line with expectations. If one side pushes too much for its own end, the chances of achieving a win-win situation will diminish. Therefore, both sides must be satisfied with the compromises they make.

In terms of compromise, the organisation must be committed to making genuine efforts to improve in line with what has been agreed. Therefore, it should only commit to initiatives that it is sure can be achieved. Failure to meet a commitment may be viewed as having made empty promises, which may destroy trust and the relationship, leaving activists with a negative view of the company.

If unsure as to whether certain steps are feasible, the organisation should admit this, stating why it does not know, how it intends to find out and when it should have an answer. (Such situations highlight the benefit of the involvement of an independent third-party expert.) When a commitment is made, a clear outline of the time frame involved should be given. Organisations should never over-promise. Under-promising slightly allows a little breathing space – better to be seen as exceeding commitments rather than failing to meet them.

---

[4] Dozier D M *et al* (1995) *Managers' Guide to Excellence in Public Relations and Communication Management*, Lawrence Erlbaum Associates, New Jersey

KEEPING NEGOTIATIONS ON COURSE

To ensure that progress is being made and being seen to be made, organisations should keep focused on the objectives of negotiation. Prior to each meeting, realistic objectives for that meeting should be set. Improvements that have been made by the organisation should be documented so they can be discussed in detail at the meeting. At the close of each meeting, further objectives should be set.

In between meetings, keeping the lines of communication open by phone or e-mail is to be recommended as it increases interaction between both sides in a less formal atmosphere. Any issues, questions or concerns that arise can be discussed. As the relationship develops, ad hoc communication may extend to informing activists of relevant information such as news stories that might be of interest. However, the organisation should also respect activists' time by ensuring items are of relevance.

TREADING WITH CAUTION

Organisations should be sensitive to the fact that activists' views can change depending on issues that arise. No matter what state the relationship is at or how comfortable things might appear, there is always a need to tread carefully. For example, an international group such as Greenpeace may have good relations with a company in one country but may have problems with it in another, drawing international attention to the organisation affecting all regions. Having said that, one of the benefits of building relations with international groups is that an operation in one country may get an early warning signal that the company may be a target elsewhere and may advise its international counterparts.

Another case for caution is in informing broader audiences of how the organisation works with activists. Should organisations wish to inform key audiences of progress being made in cooperation with an activist group, they should first discuss this with members of the group. Failure to do so may leave activists feeling compromised and used. If relations between both sides are good and real progress has been made, activists should not have a problem with broader audiences being informed. However, they may have input on how this should be done and may wish, where relevant (eg to the media), to make the announcement jointly.

Mutual cooperation can be highlighted verbally as part of ongoing relationship building with key audiences and in a broader sense through brochures, leaflets, Web sites and the media. Should activists wish to keep their involvement confidential, the organisation can still proceed in letting the public know about improvements it has made to its facilities. Information provided should be easy to understand and should be factual rather than promotional.

INVOLVING ACTIVISTS AND POTENTIAL ACTIVISTS IN DECISION MAKING

Involving activists in organisational decision making will, for many, seem idealistic. However, there are many real benefits to be accrued from this approach.

The benefits of involving activists

- People who are involved in the making of decisions are more likely to accept the outcomes of these decisions. Therefore, activists and potential activists (eg community groups) are more likely to agree with organisational activities, such as the expansion of a plant or the introduction of an incineration process, if they have been involved in planning and deciding on them.
- Obtaining the views of people outside the organisation can make for more open discussion, taking into consideration a broader range of views. This is more likely to result in better decisions that are more likely to be acceptable to a broader range of people, in particular, people outside the organisation.
- Involving activists in the decision-making process is an example of how an organisation can genuinely meet its commitment to work together with groups to improve its functioning. In being involved in decision making, members of activist groups are turned into stakeholders. Their views are sought and considered, improving the relationship-building process significantly and helping to build trust.

● Involving activists means that they are more likely to under-stand the position the organisation is in and the limitations it faces, as well as to recognise that it is genuinely working to improve the situation.

Looking back on the lessons that they learnt from the Brent Spar incident, Shell have said[5] that they should have consulted with a wider range of groups prior to finalising plans for the disposal of the oil rig.

How to involve groups

There are many ways to involve groups in the decision-making process.

One-to-one

The simplest and easiest way to involve groups in decision making is to seek their views at the embryonic stage of planning. So, for example, if management at a manufacturing plant were planning an expansion, they would seek the views of groups as soon as the need for expansion became apparent. Ideally, groups will be offered viable expansion options and together both sides can work towards an option that satisfies all. These negotiations can take place through communications structures already in place, ie scheduled six- to eight-weekly meetings being held as part of the relationship-building process.

Depending on the views of the group, the frequency of meetings may need to be increased for a time until both sides have come to agree on a way forward. It may be that activists agree with plans and give them their full support. However, it is more likely that they will have concerns that need to be taken into consideration – thus the importance of early consultation. The process is moved forward through two-way symmetrical communications and negotiation, ideally involving a third-party arbitrator with exper-tise in the area.

Task forces

Another option is to establish a task force to oversee a project from

---

[5] Seymour, M and Moore, S (2000) *Effective Crisis Management*, Cassell, London

the planning stage. The task force would include representatives from a number of key audiences including the organisation, activists, local community, academia, etc. It may be chaired by a key person from the organisation; however, it is usually preferable to choose as unbiased an individual as possible, eg an academic. In this way, the organisation cannot be accused of being strongly involved in decision making.

Various viable options would be presented to the group at the outset. Members would meet regularly to hammer out the pros and cons of each option among themselves and would seek expert opinion at any stage if anything needed further investigation. In the end, members would vote on the least objectionable option. The task force may have certain additional stipulations that may need to be discussed with the organisation, eg certain environmental requirements in the construction of an extension to blend it in with surroundings.

The rationale behind using a task force is that organisational decisions have implications for a broader audience than just activists and that all concerned groups should be involved in the decision-making process. The views of all audiences are taken into consideration simultaneously and ironed out there and then without the organisation having to negotiate with each one of its concerned audiences individually. Such one-to-one negotiations can prove extremely difficult as each group has its own concerns that may clash with those of others. It will be next to impossible to keep all audiences happy and there will be much to-ing and fro-ing. On the other hand, when all groups get together, concerns are prioritised without the organisation having to make the unpopular decision to do so. The ultimate decision is likely to have broadest appeal.

CASE STUDY: THE BENEFITS OF TASK FORCES[6]

North West Water Ltd (NWW) delivers on average 2,000 million litres of water a day to 2.9 million customers in the north-west of England, and through its sewer network, it takes away, then treats their wastewater, making it clean before returning it to the environment. As part of a major cleanup of the coastline of north-west England, a wastewater

---

[6] Interview and ongoing correspondence (summer 2000) with Shanthi Rasaratnam, who was Special Projects Manager at NWW at the time this case history occurred

scheme was planned in 1988 to serve the whole of the Fylde coastline, stretching 20 miles, from Preston, through Blackpool (the premier coastal resort in the country) and northwards to Fleetwood. NWW was responsible for locating and building facilities in order to meet European Union regulatory bathing water requirements enforced by the Environmental Agency (EA), the UK government's environmental regulatory body.

The original planned scheme was based on the then widely accepted concept of marine treatment which involves partially treating waste-water and taking it 5 km out to sea where natural elements complete the breakdown process. Despite the fact that scientific analysis had shown this to be an effective method of treatment and the fact that the Environmental Agency had approved the plans, NWW faced major objections to both the level of treatment planned and the location of the plant. Through public exhibitions along the coast, meetings with pressure groups and local authorities, NWW tried to persuade objectors of the benefits of the plan. However, local people were sceptical about the analysis and were concerned that bacteria from partially treated water might be swept back to the shore. They demanded full biological treatment and disinfecting of discharges. The local authority refused planning permission of the company's proposals, referring them to the Department of the Environment (DoE) for determination in 1990.

One-and-a half years later, as the company continued to wait for the DoE to make a decision, a very relevant EU directive was passed – *The Urban Waste Water Treatment Directive 1991*. This regulation specified levels of treatment based on the size of discharges. This came at an opportune time for the government. The Minister for the Environment was able to defuse the situation by asking NWW to incorporate the requirements of this directive into the scheme in advance of the imple-mentation date of the directive. Although the directive's requirements were for full biological treatment, local people and pressure groups were unappeased and demanded that wastewater be disinfected also.

NWW proceeded to develop options incorporating full biological treatment as instructed by the DoE. The company faced major objec-tions to all of its proposals when they came into the public domain through consulting the relevant planning authority. Objectors included residents, local businesses and politicians who did not want a waste-water treatment plant in their locality, particularly as it included waste from adjoining regions. They also demanded more stringent treated effluent discharge standards. Local pressure groups such as 'Save Our Bay' were formed to oppose proposals. Local councillors and the leader of the Lancashire County Council added their support.

The fact that the north-west coastline of England is a significant tourist attraction for the country with, for example, more people each year visiting Blackpool than any other seaside resort in the United Kingdom, ensured that the issue developed national interest. Groups such as Save Our Shoreline, Surfers Against Sewage and the Marine Conservation Society embarked on campaigns to highlight the issue. Widespread national media coverage resulted. Unfortunately for the company, the EA kept a low profile. The brunt of the criticism was directed at NWW even though it was acting to meet EA regulations.

NWW tried to meet objections through persuasion. Public meetings with presentations and exhibitions were held at a number of locations in the region to explain the merits and reasoning behind the proposals including predictions from simulation models of coastal water quality meeting bathing water standards. Leaflets were produced and distributed at exhibitions. However, this had little effect in calming concerns. According to the company, 'It is very difficult to use reasoning and argument to persuade the public, because there is an inherent mistrust and perception that large companies use their considerable resources to present proposals that favour their own interests rather than those of the community at large'.

An external PR consultancy was engaged and NWW decided to adopt a more effective consultative approach, whereby responsibility for the decision-making process as to the type of scheme to be chosen and its location would be given to a group called the Fylde Forum. This group consisted of about forty representatives drawn from local authority officers, pressure groups, local councillors, MPs and statutory bodies representing Lancashire and Cumbria. While local campaigners wished to get involved, certain national special interest groups such as Surfers Against Sewage avoided involvement, preferring to seek media headlines to further their objectives.

The planning director of NWW at that time, Dennis Clegg, chaired the forum with the acceptance of the group, acting in effect in an independent capacity rather than representing the company's interest. About 12 different scheme options with different permutations were presented to the Fylde Forum by NWW and relevant background information provided on each option on an ongoing basis, eg details of costs and environmental impacts. Specific clarification sought by the group such as potential sites for treatment plants or any environmental concerns were investigated by the company and the resulting conclusions provided at subsequent meetings of the forum.

After about seven meetings over a period of about a year, the forum narrowed the options down to three. However, members were reluctant to make the final decision because the solution crossed local authority boundaries and local councillors in particular were reluctant to be associated with a scheme that might affect their own political image. They passed the final decision making back to the company.

It was a difficult decision to make because no matter what location was chosen, local people affected would object to the proposals. Finally, the outskirts of the town of Fleetwood was selected as the most suitable location based on costs, having the least environmental impact and involving the least risk of not achieving the stringent regulatory standard. Although the immediate local community was unhappy with the final decision on the location of the plant, the widespread objections faced when the company had adopted a less consultative, persuasion-oriented approach were considerably defused in relation to the wider community.

The local borough council representing Fleetwood, influenced by local pressure groups, refused planning permission for the detailed proposals for siting the treatment plant on the outskirts of Fleetwood. This was in spite of the company taking on board a number of concerns of local planners and proposing a fully covered architecturally attractive treatment plant with odour control. The decision was passed to the Department of the Environment for determination. In the summer of 1992, the Minister for the Environment called a public enquiry. The Inspector found in favour of NWW in February 1993, but imposed a series of conditions on visual aspects and odour control measures in implementing the proposals submitted in the planning application. Once the decision to go ahead was given by the planning inspector, in detailed consultation with the local planners and local councillors, NWW embarked on building an architecturally attractive plant that resembled a high quality industrial complex rather than a sewage works. Members of the Fylde Forum and the local council were encouraged to visit the site during construction and after the completion of the plant. The overall impression was extremely positive.

The company encouraged the Fylde Forum to wind down, considering its work to be complete. However, members were loath to dissolve the forum as they found it beneficial in terms of keeping them informed and involved.

This consultative forum/task force approach has since been adopted in establishing the Morecambe Bay Forum for developing a scheme for bathing waters in the Bay. The decision-making process in which a number of participants were previously members of the Fylde Forum was very successful partly due to their familiarity with the process.

In 1999, NWW suggested that the Environmental Agency take the lead in setting up a similar group to the Fylde Forum to deal with concerns over bathing water standards in the north-west of England coastal region. On this occasion, concerns revolved around local beaches continuing to fail EU standards. Pollution in the local marine environment is complex and diffused with many factors influencing water quality outside the control of NWW, such as farming practices. However, people looked to NWW as the source of the problem because it was responsible for wastewater treatment.

Based on lessons it had learnt over the years, in asking the Environment Agency to take the lead, NWW sought to avoid taking ownership of the problem and as such favoured the appointing of an outsider to chair the forum. Such a person, namely Professor Graham Ashworth, more recently an environmentalist and vice-chairman of the Tidy Britain Group, was asked to take up the mantle. At the same time, the company is involved in assisting the Environment Agency in investigating why bathing water continues to fail to meet standards.

NWW has summarised the benefits of the forum as follows:

- Much of the ownership of decision making was passed to those most concerned who took an active part in the thinking and decision-making process.
- The company was regarded as open and transparent and could not be accused of 'going behind backs'.
- Much opposition was diffused as people were allowed to vent their feelings at meetings.
- Objectors argued among themselves at forum meetings rather than all argument being directed at the company.
- Objectors, by being responsible for decision making, realised the difficult, effectively no-win situation NWW was in.
- The process moved forward at more speed than if the company had been left to make the decision faced with objection from all quarters.
- Objections narrowed from broad issues such as the type of scheme to focus more on its location. In the end, objections were mainly from local people in Fleetwood who did not want a treatment plant in their own backyard.

Co-opting activists on to management boards

Few companies have gone as far as to co-opt activists on to their board of management. However, doing so is an option to consider as the ultimate commitment to involving activists in decision making. It demonstrates to activists and broader audiences that the organisation is open to the views of all groups, even critics. If an organisation decides to take this brave step, it is advisable to have built relations with the group already and know that representatives are willing to work together.

SUMMARY

- Relationship building, negotiation and conflict resolution make up the cornerstone of dealing with activists.
- The ideal time to approach groups is as soon as possible, ideally before they have developed views on the organisation.
- Approaching a less hostile group first means that a learning curve can be built up on how to negotiate with activists. It may also lead to knowledge of other groups and even introductions to more hostile groups.
- Organisations benefit from trying to get inside the heads of activists. In doing so, they are in for fewer surprises such as the initial scepticism they are likely to be met with.
- Thought should be given to the way in which initial contact is made with groups. Being introduced by a mutual contact, for example, is perhaps the least threatening and suspicious method.
- An initial objective of relationship building should be for both sides to develop an understanding of each other and to accept each other's views, ie 'hedging'.
- Employing the services of an independent expert to analyse the feasibility of proposals should help lessen confrontation and suspicion, helping to move the process forward.
- Involving activists and potential activists in decision making increases the likelihood that they will accept final decisions.
- Genuine efforts should be made by the organisation to improve. In doing so, this helps progress the relationship towards a win–win situation that is of mutual benefit to both sides.
- Organisations should never get complacent about their relationship with groups as situations change.

7

When activists will not negotiate

This chapter deals with the eventuality that activists may not wish to negotiate with organisations.

WHY ACTIVISTS MAY REFUSE TO NEGOTIATE

There are a few possible reasons why activists may refuse to negotiate, including:

- Activists may be suspicious of organisational motives.
- They may not see any benefit in negotiation, considering it a waste of time.
- They may not wish to be distracted from a strategy of using high profile campaigns to increase profile, funding and membership, especially if they have had success in the past using such strategies.
- They may have entrenched views that are non-negotiable, eg certain animal rights groups will not be satisfied unless they put a complete halt to animal research.

Considering the first three reasons why activists may reject dialogue, it is clear that there is a need to explain the intention of negotiation openly and clearly, ie to work together to improve organisational performance and the relationship between both sides. Reassurance that the organisation's intentions are genuine can be provided by making initial contact through an independent third party who is known to both sides and who can explain the organisation's intentions from a neutral viewpoint. It can also be helpful to explain the potential benefits of negotiation for activists (as outlined in Chapter 3).

If a meeting is arranged, it is crucial to stick to two-way symmetrical communications (as outlined in Chapter 6), resisting the temptation to persuade. It is also important to avoid being too technical. Involving an independent arbitrator at this stage can be advantageous in moving the process forward.

Hostile groups require a special approach and will be dealt with later in this chapter.

MOVE FORWARD WITH OTHER GROUPS

If a group steadfastly resists dialogue, or if the first meeting ends in deadlock, the temptation to quit should be fought. In the short term, other groups may be approached with a view to reverting to the uncooperative group at a more appropriate time. In this way:

● Experience of negotiating with activists can be developed with groups willing to explore this option.
● Progress can be made as the organisation starts to improve its performance in negotiation with activists.
● The organisation can highlight these improvements to key audiences such as employees, opinion leaders, media contacts, decision-makers, government and relevant politicians. This supports its reputation should an uncooperative group attack before the organisation can build relations.
● Through relationship building with other groups, valuable information can be gleaned on the uncooperative group so that a future approach can be made from a more informed position.
● Groups that do negotiate with the organisation may facilitate an eventual introduction to an uncooperative group at an

appropriate time. Details of progress made through negotiation may provide reassurance that the organisation's intentions are genuine and that further progress can be made.

● The relationship-building process that has taken place is likely to reduce the risk of universal condemnation by activists in the event of an emergency. Key audiences are also likely to see the organisation as open, accountable and seeking to improve its functioning.

When real progress has been made with other groups, the uncooperative group can be approached again armed with proof that the organisation's intentions are genuine.

BUILDING DEFENCES

If groups persist in refusing to negotiate, the organisation needs to protect itself from attack. A proactive campaign of ongoing meetings involving two-way dialogue should be embarked on with key audiences. These include opinion leaders, media contacts, community members, government, regulatory bodies, investors, etc. The aim is to build an appreciation of the efforts and progress that the organisation has made at improving performance, exceeding regulations and guidelines, reducing risk, working with concerned groups, communicating risk, repeatedly seeking to meet with uncooperative groups, etc. The organisation needs to be seen to be acting responsibly. This is crucial to strengthen its reputation in the event of an activist attack.

The two-way communications programme may be supported with literature such as progress reports, fact sheets, information leaflets, etc that document progress. Web sites provide another useful means of relaying this information. The North West Water Web site, (www.nww.com) for example, details its commitments to improve and how it works with groups to ensure that its improvements are relevant. Information should be outlined in simple layman's terms and should be factual rather than self-congratulatory. Exaggerating the impact of initiatives, for example, can incur the wrath of activists.

Further advice on positioning an organisation optimally in anticipation of an activist attack can be found in Chapters 8–11 which deal with risk communications, community relations, media relations and preparing for emergencies. All of these activities should be ongoing and initiated in any case as a matter of course. However, they become even more important when groups are uncooperative or hostile.

DEALING WITH HOSTILE GROUPS

The bad news is that there exist hostile groups with entrenched views that refuse to compromise for anyone. The good news is that these are in a minority. They include extremists such as certain animal rights protesters who believe that the end justifies the means. As in the case of Stop Huntingdon Animal Cruelty (SHAC) discussed in Chapter 1, they may not be satisfied unless they shut down the organisations they target.[1] Most activists, including many other animal rights groups, shun aggressive and violent behaviour. Militant groups are the exception rather than the rule.

Should one approach hostile groups?

In approaching hostile groups there is a danger that one may simply draw attention to the organisation as a possible future target and provide sensitive information that may be used to fuel an attack. On the other hand, completely ignoring such groups leaves the organisation vulnerable to surprise attack.

Deciding whether or not to approach hostile groups will be made easier if as much is known about them as possible. A thorough research programme is key in identifying which hostile groups present a militant danger and which do not. One very effective way of getting an inside track on hostile activists is through building relations with other non-hostile groups with the same interest. Once relations have been established with more cooperative groups, their advice can be sought as to whether or not to approach the hostile group and, if so, how best to go about it.

---

[1] Ward, A (2000) 'How Animal Rights Group Hit Company in the Pocket: Pressure on fund managers may have sparked the plummeting price of shares in a research laboratory', *Financial Times*, 14 February

If approaching...

The benefits of approaching apparently hostile groups include:

- they may not be as hostile as you think;
- there may be a way forward – you would not know unless you try;
- if things do not work out, it is advantageous to be able to say to key audiences and publicly that you tried.

If a decision is taken to approach such groups, the organisation should be intimately familiar with them and know that it has something genuine to offer in terms of meeting their likely demands. Because of the potential explosiveness of the situation, the initial contact should be made through either a neutral third party or a representative of an activist group that the organisation has relations with (assuming that this group is willing and that the hostile group does not look on it negatively).

The involvement of a neutral third party with relevant expertise should help in the negotiation process if this is agreeable to the group. Two-way symmetrical communications should be embarked on as outlined in Chapter 6; however, care should be taken to avoid revealing sensitive information until the organisation is satisfied that the activist group is committed to working together.

Knowing when to end negotiations

It is useful, prior to embarking on a programme of relationship building, to decide what constitutes a deadlock in negotiations. The following situations are likely indicators of a logjam in the development of two-way symmetrical communications:

- failure by the group to accept that the organisation may not be able to meet all its demands totally and immediately;
- failure by the group to see any benefit in the organisation's genuine commitment to meeting as many of its demands as possible, as quickly as possible;
- rigidity of the group in sticking totally to unrealistic expectations;
- an unwillingness by the group to work with the organisation to implement improvements;

- an attack on the organisation despite its attempts to build relations.

When logjams are met, the organisation can do its utmost to move the process forward, the most useful method being to involve independent arbitrators. However, if no progress can be made despite these attempts, (especially if the organisation is attacked by the group), it needs to consider ending relationship-building attempts and reallocating resources to defence mechanisms as outlined below.

Defence mechanisms

Because there is a strong possibility that relationships with hostile groups may fail, organisations should have the following safety mechanisms in place before approaching these groups:

- relationship building with other relevant activist groups and the community;
- a comprehensive media relations programme;
- an ongoing programme of two-way symmetrical communications with key audiences such as opinion leaders, government, key politicians, regulatory bodies, employees, etc;
- a risk communications programme;
- a well-practised crisis management plan.

If not approaching...

These same safety nets should also be in place should the organisation decide not to approach such groups. In addition, as no attempt is to be made to work with the group, the organisation should try to avoid incurring its wrath by trying to run its operation as much as is possible in line with the wishes of such groups. It should highlight (through the media, Web site, company publications such as annual reports, newsletters, leaflets, etc) factually, rather than boastfully, positive steps it has taken, is taking and will take, to improve its functioning.

If attacked

If an organisation is attacked by a militant group that will not negotiate, it is particularly important to try to control the flow of information in an effort to minimise damage to the organisation's reputation. If the group has broken the law, the proper authorities and the media should be informed. The support of a range of relevant independent third parties should be sought to admonish the activities of the group publicly. Activists who break the law or threaten organisations with violence can and should be portrayed as such.

At the same time the organisation should not shy away from talking about the activities it carries out. For example, if it carries out research on animals, it should openly talk about this. If it fails to do so, people will suspect that there is something to hide. Being open is, of course, significantly easier to do on an ongoing proactive basis. However, if this has not been done and a group attacks, speed in reaching the media with clear messages is crucial. The following type of information can be provided:

- factual details of all the activities carried out by the group (eg arson attacks) and their implications;
- details on the organisation's activities, for example:
  - Details of the research carried out (if you do not reveal it the group will).
  - We take the following steps to ensure that animals are given the best possible care...
  - Staff who look after animals are trained vets and are there to ensure that things are done properly.
  - Research on animals is required for our industry (eg pharmaceuticals) because...
  - We realise the concerns of people and take the following steps to ensure that we carry out our activities to the highest possible standards...
  - We encourage outside regulators to supervise our operations and invite animal rights activists to get involved when we make decisions about our activities.
  - We have reviewed all the possible options to the research we carry out and have made the following improvements...
  - We will continue to review our work as new innovations and techniques are developed.
  - We work with the following animal rights groups to try to ensure the best situation for animals...
  - The following authorities support our work...

- The results of animal research have meant... (eg less suffering, illness and death in the human and animal world).
- This work has to be carried out. If we do not do it, others who care less, in countries with much more relaxed regulations, will.

Organisations should always be familiar with the typical arguments put forward by activists targeting their field of work. They must know how to answer these arguments in order to be prepared for media interrogation. Needless to say, it is much easier to convince the media, public, opinion leaders and activists of your arguments if you do so proactively, on an ongoing basis. If you are open and hide nothing, what will activists be able to highlight that people do not already know?

A case study by Center and Jackson[2] outlines how one organisation, a US university, coped with a malicious attack by animal rights extremists.

CASE STUDY: RAPID RESPONSE TO A MALICIOUS ATTACK

Universities that carry out animal research are often the subject of attacks from animal rights activists. In 1991, Oregon State University fell foul of an attack by the Animal Liberation Federation (ALF), involving arson, vandalism, flooding, destruction of records and property. The challenge to communicators was to control the media's reporting of the story by trying to beat activists in releasing information so that the university's side could be presented first, lessening the risk of being painted as cruel to animals by the media, as was the plan of the ALF.

Working in the university's favour was the fact that it had been prepared for such a situation. For example, it had a crisis management plan that it rolled out immediately. This included prepared media information on animal rights, the university's procedures and research facilities involving the care and use of animals.

A news management team was quickly established and the following media relations objectives identified:

---

[2] Center, A H and Jackson, P (1995) *Public Relations Practices*, 5th edn, Prentice-Hall, New Jersey

- to control the flow of information to the media quickly and proactively so as to manage the event;
- to establish the university as the credible and accurate source of information about the event;
- to speak with one consistent voice to the media and public;
- to ensure that the occurrence of illegal acts (arson, vandalism, destruction of property) was not overshadowed by accusations of animal rights abuses.

A notice was distributed to the media by 8.00 am, just two hours after the news and communications services director was informed of the incident by the police. The media were informed that further information would follow as soon as possible. A team of communicators went to the scene of the attack (which was located far from the campus) to gather information and assist the police, fire brigade and media. They kept in contact with the office by mobile phone. One member of the team photographed the scene and organised rapid processing of prints to facilitate media requests.

A university spokesperson was identified and briefed by the news team and made available for interview and comment. Regular news updates were sent to the media focusing on the violent and extreme acts committed by the activists such as the destruction of property that had been paid for by public funds. By 11.30 am on the same day, three updated news reports had been issued and the following key audiences informed: other universities in Oregon, federal agencies and associations and the national news media.

The speedy response by the university succeeded in beating the ALF to the media as the group's plan had been to distribute a video of its members in the process of vandalising the research centre together with a press release to the Associated Press and television studios in Portland by mid-morning. By that time the media were already familiar with the story because of the university's communications. On the whole, news coverage was positive for the university with many editorials favouring its involvement in animal experiments.

The news management team was also involved in the preparation of materials supporting testimony before a state legislative committee that was considering passing a more stringent animal rights vandalism bill. Following the testimony of university spokespeople, the bill, which made acts of animal rights vandalism a felony rather than a misdemeanour, was enacted by the 1991 Oregon Legislative Assembly.

SUMMARY

- There are many reasons why groups may not wish to negotiate with organisations. Persistence in clearly explaining intentions and making initial contact through a trusted mutual contact can overcome many initial objections.
- If a group is uncooperative, the following benefits accrue from approaching cooperative groups first, before reverting to the uncooperative group:
  - experience of negotiating with activists can be built up;
  - progress can be made in improving performance in cooperation with activists;
  - organisational improvements can be highlighted to key audiences;
  - information can be gleaned on the uncooperative group;
  - cooperative groups may lead to introductions to uncooperative ones;
  - in an emergency, universal activist condemnation is less likely.
- Organisations need to protect themselves against attack from hostile groups through building relations with key audiences (eg government, opinion leaders, employees, shareholders, the media, the community, etc) in order to achieve recognition for being responsible in their functioning.
- There are risks associated with approaching militant groups. Research is crucial in identifying which groups are militant and which are not. In deciding whether or not to approach such groups, the advice of activists working with the organisation should be sought.
- Regardless of whether or not groups are approached, the following safety nets should be put in place if hostile groups prove a threat:
  - relationship building with less hostile groups;
  - an advanced media relations programme;
  - relationship building with key audiences;
  - a well-practised crisis management plan;
  - a risk communications programme.
- If approaching hostile groups, the organisation should have an in-depth knowledge of the groups and the likelihood and extent of being able to meet their demands. Initial contact should be made through a mutual contact. Involving an inde-

pendent arbitrator is also to be recommended. Two-way symmetrical communications should be employed and caution is needed in revealing sensitive information at the initial stages. The organisation should be prepared to cease efforts at dialogue if logjams cannot be overcome.

8

Communicating about risk

When involved in a business that entails risk such as accidental toxic spillage, there is a temptation to gloss over risks when communicating with key audiences. This chapter highlights the dangers of this approach and outlines why and how organisations can benefit from communicating about the risks associated with their business.

DANGERS OF KEEPING QUIET ABOUT RISKS

Staying quiet about risks is itself a risk, for the following reasons:

- If an organisation is involved in a business that has inherent risks, it is likely that most of its key audiences will be aware of this. If an organisation does not discuss risk and seeks to reassure audiences, people are likely to have concerns.
- Those concerned about risks are even more likely to worry if an organisation keeps quiet about risks because:

- they may reason that the organisation will not discuss risk because it is hiding something really big;
- they may worry that the organisation is not taking the risk sufficiently seriously and is not working hard enough to reduce risk;
- risks that are not understood are feared more.[1]

- Those with concerns are likely to mistrust and resent an organisation that does not listen to and address their concerns. If an organisation refuses to admit the risks that are associated with its business, concerned citizens are more likely to organise to do something to force the company to reduce the risk.

- Activists often exaggerate the risks associated with an organisation. People are more likely to believe activists' claims if the organisation has not been communicating openly with them and a lack of trust exists.

- Once people fear risk it is very difficult to reduce that fear,[2] particularly if activists are working to heighten it.

- Failure to communicate risk can leave an organisation open to litigation, boycotts and public debate when, following an incident, it is accused of having concealed risks.[3]

UNDERSTANDING RISK

To explain why it is advisable to communicate about risk it is useful to examine the concept of risk.

The degree of concern people have about risks is not based on logical, scientific fact. The greatest threats to our existence, for example, do not frighten us as much as things that pose significantly less risk. Briefly, people fear risk more if they do not understand it, do not take it voluntarily, feel they have no control over it, do not trust the organisation presenting it or believe the consequences of the risk to be severe. Communicating about risk, termed 'risk communications', seeks to reduce concerns proac-

---

[1] Blood, R (1996) 'Psychology, Pressure Groups and Environmentalism', *Journal of Communication Management*, **1** (1), pp 51–58, Henry Stewart Publications, London

[2] Sandman, P M (1993) *Responding to Community Outrage: Strategies for effective risk communication*, American Industrial Hygiene Association Press, Fairfax

[3] Wilcox, D L *et al* (1997) *Public Relations Strategies and Tactics*, 5th edn, Longman, New York

tively by being open about and seeking to build an understanding of risk. Where possible, audiences are involved in decision making. This increases their control over the risk, in an effort to increase the acceptability of the risk.

THE BASIC PRINCIPLES OF RISK COMMUNICATIONS

Risk communications involves:

- an ongoing process of two-way symmetrical communications to seek to identify concerns;
- listening to and accepting these concerns no matter how illogical they may seem;
- apologising for the risks;
- seeking to address concerns, openly and honestly by:
  - explaining risks and putting them into perspective;
  - highlighting that the organisation is also concerned about risks and has taken precautions to reduce them (these need to be detailed);
  - outlining that the organisation is monitored and regulated by named authorities;
  - explaining the steps the organisation will take in the event of emergencies, including informing people.
- preparing to deal with negative reactions through conflict resolution, where both sides seek to work together towards reducing risk;
- involving audiences in decision making about the risk, eg early input into the planning of an expansion of a manufacturing plant.

Listening to concerns

Listening to concerns affords the opportunity to learn audiences' views of the company so that an understanding of their fears can be developed. Only then can they be addressed appropriately. Once an organisation starts to listen to people's concerns, it starts to show that it cares, which is the first step in reducing fear.

Accepting fears as legitimate

Before an organisation can work to ease concerns, it has to accept the concerns of an audience as legitimate. It may help to keep in mind that people's fears are usually based, not on logic or scientific fact, but on their lack of understanding and their feelings of powerlessness to control risk. An acceptance by the organisation of people's fears as real is crucial in order to show empathy. Unless the organisation empathises, it is unlikely to be listened to. Empathy is particularly important in cases where the risk involves something that people inherently dread such as cancer.[4]

Apologising for risks

Apologising for risks can go a long way towards easing people's anger. In many cases, failure to apologise can often be seen to be one of the biggest 'crimes' committed by an organisation. In 1997, Nike inadvertently insulted Muslims by displaying on the soles of a new range of shoes, 'Summer Hoops', a logo that resembled the name of Allah. When they learnt of the problem Nike, without speaking with activists, altered the logo and made a public announcement to the effect that the issue had been dealt with. Rather than diffusing the situation, the issue escalated with critics calling the move a gesture and admonishing Nike for not apologising. The situation was diffused only when Nike, through negotiation with activists developed a 14-point agreement that served to review the incident, rectify the situation in a way that was satisfactory to Muslims and help prevent such an incident happening again.[5] Apologising is actually quite easy once one knows its effectiveness.

Explaining risks

If little is known about a risk, people tend to exaggerate it for their own self-protection. Being told there is nothing to worry about worries people more as they fear either that 1) the organisation is not taking the risk seriously and is failing to take precautions; or 2)

---

[4] Sandman, P M (1993) *Responding to Community Outrage: Strategies for effective risk communication*, American Industrial Hygiene Association Press, Fairfax
[5] Seymour, M and Moore, S (2000) *Effective Crisis Management*, Cassell, London

that the organisation is trying to cover up a very real danger by keeping quiet. Either situation increases concern.

If, on the other hand, a risk is explained, it is made more tangible. People know what they are dealing with and are reassured that the organisation is taking the risk seriously by being open and by explaining what it is doing to reduce risk proactively.

In explaining risks, an organisation needs to listen to concerns and take them into account. People need to understand why the risk exists, the level of risk involved, its implications and what the organisation is doing to prevent risks and prepare for emergencies. This is particularly important if the organisation is involved in a business that involves the risk of a catastrophic event such as an explosion, where people are more likely to fear risk.[6]

According to risk communications expert Peter Sandman, because people have a greater fear of risk if an organisation has already had a 'memorable incident' such as a chemical spill, it is best not to ignore this incident when communicating with people. This omission will only serve to anger people further as they feel the organisation is ignoring its past mistakes. Rather, the organisation should talk repeatedly about the incident and what it learnt from it to reassure people that it is doing its utmost to prevent such an incident ever happening again. Eventually audiences will tire of hearing about the incident.[7]

Putting risks into perspective

When seeking to put risks into perspective, it is often useful, where possible, to compare risks to other familiar everyday situations. For example, UK mobile phone company, One 2 One, when seeking to create an understanding of the risk associated with mobile phone masts, uses special equipment to demonstrate that there is less electromagnetic radiation from masts than commonly used appliances such as microwaves, computers, etc. Involving people in estimating risks for themselves by giving them the detector to use helps to empower them in checking risk.

Peter Sandman warns that when comparing risk, it is best to avoid comparing industrial risks with natural risks,[8] eg nuclear

---

[6] Sandman, P M (1993) *Responding to Community Outrage: Strategies for effective risk communication*, American Industrial Hygiene Association Press, Fairfax

[7] *Ibid.*

[8] *Ibid.*

power versus the risk of developing skin cancer from overexposure to the sun. According to Sandman, this argument is likely to backfire, as people do not compare natural and industrial risks on the same level and may see the organisation as trying to play God. This builds resentment.

In putting risks into perspective, organisations should be honest about the level of risk. Over-minimising risk is even worse than failing to adopt a risk communications programme, as it misleads people about risk and leaves the organisation open to activist attack, litigation, public criticism, etc.

Explaining the organisation's concern and commitment

People are more likely to believe an organisation that communicates that it is concerned about the risks associated with its business than one that states that it is unconcerned. Once an organisation says openly that it is concerned about risks *and* that it is actively taking steps to reduce them, audiences are more likely to believe and trust it. This approach is more likely to instil confidence in the public that the organisation is both responsive and responsible. If an incident does occur, key audiences will know that the organisation had done its best to prevent it by reducing risks.

Explaining monitoring and regulations

In addition to communicating the steps the organisation voluntarily takes to reduce risk, it is further reassuring to outline how the organisation is independently monitored and regulated. For example, a chemical manufacturer regulated by an environmental protection agency could explain that if it plans any new procedures, these have to be reviewed by the agency and approved before plans can go ahead. Brief, easy-to-understand details of the relevant bodies should be given to provide reassurance as to their credibility and independence.

Explaining emergency procedures

People fear emergencies. As part of the risk communications process, an organisation needs to reassure people of the steps that it will take in the event of an emergency. The organisation must be honest about the implications of an emergency. People need to know what to expect. The organisation needs to explain the procedures that it has in place that will be implemented in the event of an emergency. If it regularly carries out dry runs of possible emergencies (eg fire drills) this should be communicated with audiences. It is also important to reassure that the organisation will be open in its communications during an emergency, eg informing the local community, media and other key audiences immediately of the situation.

Preparing for negative reactions

All of the above aspects of risk communications need to be implemented in tandem. For example, highlighting risks without putting them into perspective or explaining what the organisation is doing to prevent them will simply serve to worry people. Nevertheless, when embarking on a risk communications programme an organisation should prepare to deal with negative reactions through dialogue and conflict resolution.

Involving audiences in decision making

People are less outraged by risks if they have a degree of control over the risk.[9, 10] For example, people fear mobile phones less than mobile phone masts as they can control how much they use their phone. Increasing people's control of risks is one solution to reducing their perception of risk. This can be done by sharing the decision-making process through advisory boards, task forces, external audits of the organisation, co-opting activists onto boards of management, etc.

---

[9] Sandman, P M (1993) *Responding to Community Outrage: Strategies for effective risk communication*, American Industrial Hygiene Association Press, Fairfax
[10] Wilcox, D L *et al* (1997) *Public Relations Strategies and Tactics*, 5th edn, Longman, New York

CASE STUDY: PUBLIC BACKLASH AGAINST PERCEIVED FAILURE TO COMMUNICATE[11]

In 1994, a UK-based building products supplier faced opposition to a new fuel it had begun to use in its manufacturing process. The factory had been operating for about 70 years using one type of fuel. It had not faced opposition and had good relations with the local community. In 1992, it changed from using coal, a natural resource, to a fuel based on waste material. The rationale was that in doing so, a natural resource was not being used up. Rather, waste that had previously been disposed of in landfill was now being used productively in the manufacture of building materials. The new fuel was also considerably less expensive than coal.

The company informed local community representatives of its decision. It did not receive any objection until two years later when the community at large learnt of the change. Knowing little about the new fuel and worried that it was more toxic than coal, members of the community began to object. Their main source of outrage was that they felt that they had not been consulted. They felt that the company had tried to sneak the new process in through the back door.

Individuals began to organise into groups. They called public meetings and informed the local media of their concerns. Anecdotal evidence including incidences of health problems such as asthma attacks were highlighted. Concerns escalated. Friends of the Earth became involved. All groups, regardless of size, proved powerful in negatively impacting on the company's reputation.

What began as a local issue quickly became a national one as the national media became involved. The issue became self-perpetuating – media coverage increased awareness of the problem, which resulted in more letters to the editor and more stories. If a journalist was doing a feature, for example on toxic waste, because this case had such a high profile, it was top of the mind and easy to include in the article as a case history, contacting local groups for their comment. Importantly, the company involved has said that the majority of national press journalists writing articles did not consult them and that misinformation was widespread. The company has since faced years of objection and negative coverage.

Interestingly, the Internet proved a major problem in this case. Information generated on the Web provided the 'factual' basis for much of the objection. This was taken at face value and seldom questioned. The organisation found it extremely difficult to respond.

---

[11] Case history developed through interview and liaison with the public relations officer of the company in question, which wishes to remain anonymous

Because the exact source of the information was unclear, it was intangible and difficult to argue with.

Though the company had been given the authority to use the waste fuel by its regulatory authority and had evidence that it had no greater environmental impact than coal, because people perceived they had not been informed and because objection was so widespread, the organisation was not listened to or believed. The company thought its problems were over when a £500,000 study carried out by its regulatory body revealed that air quality was not adversely affected by burning the new fuel. Unfortunately, public opinion of the organisation was so strongly negative at this stage that objectors turned on the regulatory body accusing it of failing to be impartial.

The company admits that this issue did spoil relations with the community and affected trust that had been built up over 70 years. Good relations are very quick to crumble under pressure. Rebuilding them has proven a mammoth task. However, much has been learnt from the experience, including the following:

- *It is a mistake to think that you are creating an issue* by talking about it. People find out in the end, and when they do they are outraged because they were not informed. More than anything else, this outrage will spur them into action.
- *Early consultation is crucial.* Plans need to be discussed before people begin to object. Once a campaign against an organisation goes ahead, it can take on a life of its own. Few people will listen to or believe the company. Years later the issue can reappear in the media – just when you were beginning to think it had gone away.
- *Widespread consultation is crucial.* You cannot rely on representatives to spread the news – you have to do so yourself and employ a strategy to do so. This company, having learnt from its experience, when subsequently planning an expansion at another operation embarked on a widespread consultation campaign involving focus group meetings, newsletters, a freephone number, comment line, etc. Objection was significantly less.
- *You cannot beat face-to-face dialogue.* The company learnt that the most successful approach to dealing with objection (if you do fail to prevent it in the first place) is through face-to-face dialogue with both pressure groups and the community. While some more hostile groups might refuse to meet, this company has found that meeting face-to-face makes the company seem human. Rather than dealing with an anonymous company, the public is meeting real people.
- *Open days work.* One of the most successful approaches taken by this company was to hold an open day. Employees mixed openly and socially with 1,500 attendees. Many of the employees were

local people with much in common with community members and objectors. People could see the manufacturing process for themselves, reassuring them that the company was professional, reducing fear of the unknown.

- *Public meetings can prove difficult.* This company has learnt through its experience that public meetings can act as a sounding box for more militant groups and individuals. However, if others are holding a public meeting, it is advantageous to attend, so as to avoid appearing to be hiding from the issue. Questions can be addressed there and then.
- *Better to be transparent – warts and all.* Through its experiences, this company has learnt that openness is a must. Because it operates in a 'heavy industry', it is occasionally prosecuted. When this occurs, it publicly announces this in press releases and newsletters, etc. The news comes from them, not someone else. Transparency builds trust.
- *Media relations.* Building contacts with local media and facilitating the national media have proven important for this company in terms of seeking more balanced coverage. They have also avoided getting involved in tit-for-tat letters to the editor as this prolongs issues. A media relations programme has meant that the media have begun to contact the company before writing articles to check their facts. In some cases, the public relations officer (PRO) has managed to convince journalists against writing certain articles on the organisation. In this regard, face-to-face contact with journalists was crucial with the PRO personally visiting the journalists' papers to talk with them.

AT WHAT STAGE SHOULD RISK COMMUNICATIONS BE COMMENCED?

The sooner an organisation discusses risk the better – it is easier to communicate risk in a 'neutral opinion environment' when audiences have not made up their minds on the organisation or the issue.[12] An individual's perception of the size of risk is dependent on when and how information about risk is received. If the organisation takes control of communication about risk by proactively discussing it and the steps taken to reduce risk, there is an opportunity to explain the full context of the risk. If an organi-

---

[12] Alison Clark, DVisions Ltd, Hove

sation remains quiet about risk, it becomes vulnerable to activists who seek to highlight, if not exaggerate, risks, claiming that the organisation had been deliberately trying to conceal them. This magnifies risks even further and presents the organisation as considerably less trustworthy. In this environment, explaining risk becomes considerably more difficult as opinions are polarised – see Figure 8.1.

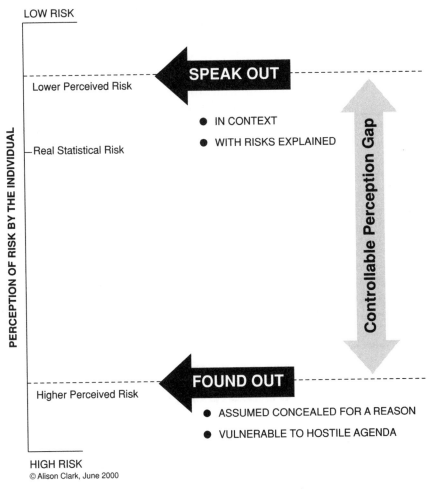

Figure 8.1 *Managing the perception gap*

WHO TO COMMUNICATE RISK TO

The key audiences that risk should be communicated to include:

- activists and potential activists;
- employees;
- the local community;
- regulators;
- politicians;
- experts in the field, ie opinion leaders;
- the media;
- members of the public who are concerned.

Care is needed when communicating risk with activists and the media as there is always the possibility that facts and figures may be sensationalised. Risk communications with both of these audiences should be done as part of an ongoing process of relationship building. Relationship building with key people in the media is discussed in Chapter 10.

With the benefit of hindsight, Shell oil company has published various lessons it has learnt from the Brent Spar disposal incident.[13] The company regrets not having employed genuine two-way communications with a wider audience, underestimating public interest in the issue and failing to take people's emotional reactions into consideration. Shell's public affairs manager has also highlighted the importance of genuinely listening to, appreciating and responding to people's fears and emotions.

WHEN TO EMPLOY RISK COMMUNICATIONS

Many organisations that did not perceive their operations to pose much risk have been taken by surprise when activists incited public fear of their activities. They were even more surprised when the public would not listen to their reassurances. Even if the experts reassure an organisation that its activities pose little risk, it

---

[13] Seymour, M and Moore, S (2000) *Effective Crisis Management*, Cassell, London

is useful for organisations to refer to 12 questions Peter Sandman[14] poses which help to identify how the public might perceive their operation in terms of risk:

PETER SANDMAN'S QUESTIONS TO ASK IN RISK COMMUNICATIONS

1. Is it voluntary or coerced?
2. Is it natural or industrial?
3. Is it familiar or exotic?
4. Is it not memorable or memorable?
5. Is it not dreaded or dreaded?
6. Is it chronic or catastrophic?
7. Is it knowable or not knowable?
8. Is it controlled by me or by others?
9. Is it fair or unfair?
10. Is it morally irrelevant or morally relevant?
11. Can I trust you or not?
12. Is the process responsive or unresponsive?

According to Sandman, the perception of risk is greater if:

- the public does not have a choice whether or not to take the risk;
- it is industrial as opposed to naturally occurring;
- it is a risk that people are unfamiliar with or do not understand;
- people have a past experience of a 'memorable incident' associated with such a risk, eg high profile accidents such as Chernobyl or Bhopal;
- people have an inherent dread or fear of the risk, eg cancer;
- it presents a danger of catastrophe, eg an explosion;
- it is hard to quantify, if experts disagree about the level of risk or if it is difficult to detect (eg nuclear radiation);
- it is in the complete control of an organisation and the public has no input;

---

[14] Sandman, P M (1993) *Responding to Community Outrage: Strategies for effective risk communication*, American Industrial Hygiene Association Press, Fairfax

- it can be considered unfair, eg the location of a sewage works in a town that has to deal with the sewage from a much wider area;
- it is presented by an organisation that is not trusted;
- it is presented by an organisation that is secretive, unapologetic, discourteous, confrontational or dispassionate.

An organisation that recognises itself in the above description should consider the benefits of risk communications.

SUMMARY

- Not communicating about the risks associated with your business is itself a risk as it can lead to:
  - mistrust of the organisation;
  - increased public concern leading to increased risk of organised opposition;
  - exaggeration of risks by activists being believed;
  - increased risk of litigation.
- Risk causes most concern if:
  - it is not understood;
  - its consequences are severe;
  - it is not taken voluntarily;
  - it is presented by an organisation that is not trusted.
- Risk communication involves seeking to reduce concerns by listening to people who are concerned, explaining risks, highlighting what the organisation is doing to reduce risk and prevent emergencies. It also involves seeking to involve relevant audiences in decision making.
- Ideally, risk communications should begin in a 'neutral opinion environment' before audiences have made up their minds on an organisation or issue as it will be easier to put risks into perspective.
- Organisations should look to Peter Sandman's 12 factors that increase the public's perception of risk so as to identify how risky their activities are likely to be viewed rather than simply relying on the reassurances of statistics.

9

Community relations

When one considers that members of the local community living in the vicinity of an organisation have most to lose from issues such as pollution or commercial accidents, it should not be surprising that their concerns often lead them to unite in pressuring organisations to change. This chapter focuses on building relations with this key audience in an effort to prevent such situations from arising.

WHY IS THE LOCAL COMMUNITY SO IMPORTANT?

The local community should be regarded as a key audience for the following reasons:

- Their proximity to the organisation means they are often first to notice and draw public attention to issues such as pollution, noise, smells, etc.
- Because they have very real concerns for their own health and lifestyles, they tend to form extremely committed, determined and active groups.

- Their activities can stimulate the interest of special interest groups such as environmentalists, to compound the situation.
- Information travelling back and forth between company employees and family and friends in the community influences the reputation of the company.
- Whether an organisation likes it or not, it is part of a community with certain obligations that should not be ignored.

WHY DO LOCAL COMMUNITIES FORM GROUPS?

People living in the vicinity of an organisation have to do so 24 hours a day, seven days a week, 52 weeks a year. When employees go home, the local community is still there, living day and night with the organisation in its presence. If that organisation is involved in manufacture, research, mining, exploration, nuclear power, water treatment, etc, living in its presence can have wide-ranging implications. These include the unsightliness of a factory, smells, noise, emissions, contamination of water, traffic problems, inconvenience, impact on property prices and the potential for explosions, fires or chemical spills. These can cause very real concerns for the health and quality of life of all residents, particularly children. Fear unites communities to organise into pressure groups often by way of residents' associations or community groups.

Communities also organise as new threats appear on the horizon such as unwelcome organisations seeking planning permission in the community. Armed with a 'not in my backyard' (NIMBY) mentality, communities tend to fight these cases ferociously for the following reasons:

- they represent an unknown and intangible threat;
- there is an opportunity to prevent the problem – infinitely preferable to trying to control it once there;
- as industry tends to cluster together, the intended location may represent yet another threat for a community already coping with industry present – as such it may be the last straw for residents who will fight furiously to prevent it.

Many organisations feel that there is little they can do when faced with the NIMBY syndrome. They feel that because people simply do not want whatever it is the organisation wishes to 'impose' on them, there is no solution. The following case history demonstrates the potential benefits of a proactive consultation process with the local community.

CASE STUDY: FULL AND EARLY CONSULTATION FACILITATES COMMUNITY ACCEPTANCE OF SEWAGE INCINERATOR[1]

In 1993, Lothian Regional Council[2] (LRC), the water authority responsible for the east of Scotland, learnt that the method it used for disposing of sewage sludge (ie sea dumping of processed sludge), was to become illegal by the year 2001. LRC came under pressure from UK and European parliaments to have agreed and planned a new method of disposal by the end of 1998 for implementation before the close of 2001. LRC commissioned independent research into alternatives. Incineration was proposed as the most environmentally friendly option. LRC hired a public relations firm, PR Consultants Scotland (PRCS)[3] to advise on the public acceptability of this option.

Before proposing a plan of action, PRCS undertook extensive research into the following areas: practices and policies of the LRC, the approach being taken by other water authorities, the success or otherwise of incinerator operators in terms of their management of public opinion. PRCS learnt that while LRC had a strong environmental track record and sound environmental policy, potentially it faced major objection to incineration. Their research showed that wherever other UK water authorities had chosen to incinerate sewage sludge they had faced extremely strong objection, mainly from local communities who did everything in their power to drive the planning process to public enquiry. In many cases this had resulted in costly and time-consuming public enquiries and, in a number of cases, refusal of planning permission. To make matters worse, media coverage of incineration generally tended to be extremely negative.

PRCS proposed a wide scale consultation process with the community. It advised LRC to be as open as possible as early as possible in communicating about incineration generally and their plans specifically.

[1] Case history developed following interview and liaison (May/June 2000) with Claire Davidson, Chief Executive, Shandwick Consumer, Entertainment and Healthcare UK
[2] East of Scotland Water Authority now holds responsibility for the disposal of sewage in this area
[3] PRCS is now Shandwick Scotland

109

Following months of preparation (July–October 1993) that included training staff media, inviting local councillors to visit a similar incinerator in Yorkshire, the production of materials, etc, LRC rolled out its consultation programme. This took place from October 1993 to May 1994.

The consultation process kicked off with a formal launch to community leaders that included feedback mechanisms such as a question and answer session, one-to-one briefings, feedback questionnaires and the option of further one-to-one meetings within seven days to discuss any further issues or concerns. This consultation process was highlighted in the local media. The launch to community leaders was followed the next day by a media briefing and photocall. Within a week, a community newsletter had been delivered to 120,000 homes in the local area. These activities were designed to ensure that as many members of the community were informed of plans as quickly as possible.

Importantly, LRC adopted a wide range of activities designed to obtain feedback on people's views and to allow those concerned to air their objections or grievances. Immediate mechanisms to allow people to respond to initial announcements included a freephone line and 'comment sheets'. The freephone line was set up to take questions and comments – all calls were responded to within 24 hours. The existence of the line was advertised extensively. Comment sheets were widely distributed, eg at meetings, with mailings, at a mobile exhibition trailer, etc. All comments were acknowledged and answered in writing.

More in-depth consultation was facilitated through organised meetings with local community leaders, special interest groups and district and regional councillors. Twenty meetings were held over an eight-week period. Of around 2,000 individuals invited, 30 per cent attended. Non-attendees were mailed a brochure providing in-depth information on the programme, the workings of an incinerator and an independent Environmental Impact Assessment that had been carried out. At meetings, two-way dialogue was stimulated through question and answer sessions.

A mobile interactive exhibition visited 19 venues in the region during a 14-week period. The location of the trailer was advertised extensively. Special presentations to individual groups were offered as necessary. Media coverage was monitored carefully.

From May to July 1994, public response to the consultation was evaluated. Results were reported to planners and the openness of the public consultation emphasised. The planning application was approved without a public enquiry. Sir Hector Monro, MP, Minister for Agriculture and the Environment at the time summarised the public consultation programme by writing:

The extent of the consultation has included public meetings, an exhibition trailer and consultation comment sheets which were issued to 3,000 households. In all, 120,000 households were contacted and only 19 responses expressing disapproval to the proposals were received. The public have therefore been fully consulted on this environmentally sensitive project and this is very much in line with Government policy that the public should have full access to environmental information when such projects are being considered.

This case history highlights the importance of:

- research to identify potential issues;
- accepting the results of research and acting on them;
- the local community and its ability to hamper and/or halt the planning process;
- early and extensive consultation to facilitate community acceptance of projects;
- a wide and coordinated range of educational and consultation measures;
- openness both in terms of facilitating public acceptance of projects and also in aiding the planning process by being seen to have consulted audiences and gained their approval;
- proactively working to gain public acceptance of projects eases the planning process.

WINNING COMMUNITY SUPPORT

Winning community support can be very difficult.[4] If an organisation is to have any success in doing so, its management must believe in its social responsibility and consistently support two-way symmetrical communications. Once located in a community, ongoing relationship building, negotiation and conflict resolution should be initiated with local community groups in much the same way as when dealing with activists as outlined in Chapter 6. There are, however, certain specific additional issues that also need to be addressed:

1. the type of people involved;
2. breaking down barriers;

[4] Studies in Seitel, F P (1995) *The Practice of Public Relations*, 6th edn, Prentice-Hall, New Jersey

3. handling complaints;
4. interaction between employees and community;
5. the importance of risk communications;
6. communicating in emergencies;
7. liaison groups;
8. sponsorship.

The type of people involved

Organisations should remember that community members are mums, dads, children, the elderly, etc who have very real concerns that affect them personally. Their level of understanding of organisations and their activities is likely to be minimal as is their interest in such matters. They are unlikely to want to listen to technicalities about the organisation, being more interested in what can be done about a problem rather than details as to why it exists.

There is a need to be empathetic, non-technical and open when dealing with communities. Listening is crucial. An attempt should be made to speak from a common perspective, ie as members of the same community with similar concerns. The company should speak in a language that means something to the people. So, for example, rather than dwelling on detailed figures regarding emission levels that mean little, the focus should be on the fact that the organisation complies with strict guidelines and regulations. Analogies to everyday situations should be discussed such as the degree of risk from emissions compared to the generally recognised and accepted risks such as fumes from cars.

Local people need a means of discussing their concerns with the organisation. They need to be able to go to someone they know and trust within the organisation. Responsibility for ongoing community relations needs to be allocated to key staff in order to personalise the company. These individuals need to be open, approachable and helpful. It is an advantage if they are actually from the local community or live locally. Ideally, responsibility for community relations should rest with individuals responsible for dealing with activists as the same qualities, background and areas of expertise are required (see Chapter 4). Also the community may at any stage become activists.

CASE STUDY: ONE 2 ONE LEARNS IMPORTANT LESSONS IN COMMUNITY RELATIONS[5]

UK mobile phone company One 2 One has learnt many lessons in community relations since people first began to object to the location of its mobile phone masts near their homes. This issue really took off in 1998, when health concerns about electromagnetic radiation from mobile phones were raised in the US media. Two years later, One 2 One were installing between 100–160 sites per month and meeting some form of objection with approximately 20 per cent of these. At the time, their Community Relations Manager, Nick Sharples, spoke of the many important lessons in community relations the company has learnt since public concern became an issue. Among these are:

- *Identify potential issues early and convince senior management of the need to invest resources and develop skills.* Mobile phone companies first encountered significant community objection to mobile phone masts in Australia in the mid 1990s following deregulation of Telstra, the state telecoms monopoly. In hindsight, Sharples says that the mobile phone industry should have seen the writing on the wall and been more proactive in preparing for similar reactions in other countries. One 2 One did look to Australian mobile companies to help develop skills once objections occurred in the UK. This proved advantageous.
- *Try to minimise objection from the outset.* One 2 One employs agents with local knowledge who are likely to be as sensitive to the local environment as possible to choose locations for sites carefully.
- *Ensure that the community is informed and consulted about what is coming,* as people who feel they have been consulted are less likely to object. One 2 One's agents work with the local council and community groups to ensure residents and other stakeholders are well informed of plans to locate masts.
- *Listen to and empathise with the community's concerns.* One 2 One has learnt that people need to feel that their views and concerns are being considered before they will listen to the organisation, while at the same time the organisation needs to know people's concerns before they can address them.
- *Local residents are not interested in hearing technical details* – they do not want to be baffled by science – they simply do not want the problem in their backyard (the NIMBY syndrome). One 2 One's

---

[5] Interview and liaison with Nick Sharples, Community Relations Manager, One 2 One, April 2000

experience reflects many others and the company has learnt to communicate more effectively by recognising this attitude. For example, in relation to health concerns, rather than referring to studies that seem cold, clinical and distant, the company focuses on comparing the levels of radiation from mobile phone masts to common household items such as computer screens, cordless baby alarms, radio controlled toys, etc. They use an 'exposure meter' to demonstrate this, so that people can see the levels for themselves. In this way information is simplified and, importantly, personalised to relate directly to them.

- *Residents only want to hear what directly concerns them.* For example, they do not want to hear how One 2 One is improving the national mobile phone network. Rather they want to hear that they themselves will get a better service from their mobile phones if a mast is erected.

- *Learn about the community.* One 2 One has found that, in many cases, there may be one 'ringleader' in the community who is the main source of the objection and who is actively encouraging others to object. If that person is identified and communicated with on a one-to-one basis, the source of protest can usually be resolved. This usually involves visiting the person in his or her home to listen to and address his or her concerns.

- *Public meetings should be avoided.* One 2 One's experience has been that public meetings tend to revert to shouting matches where little communication is achieved on either side. When public meetings are suggested, the company proposes an alternative – an 'Open House' where company representatives make themselves available in a community room to be available on a one-to-one basis to discuss individual concerns. In this way the confrontational aspect of public meetings is avoided and two-way symmetrical communications can be adopted in a relaxed environment. Community members benefit from having their queries and concerns addressed on a personal basis.

- *Adopt risk communication techniques.* Learning and adopting these techniques have proven crucial in improving One 2 One's community relations track record.

- *Through consultation, make genuine efforts to improve.* One 2 One is continually adopting new technology to improve masts by making them slimmer and less obtrusive. Where possible, masts are camouflaged or hidden to reduce their visual impact. One 2 One has consulted environmental experts such as international environmental campaigner Professor David Bellamy to help with landscaping around masts to ensure the development of a natural habitat.

From a resources point of view, the company has highlighted the potential benefits of being able to identify situations that are likely to prove problematic early. Local newspaper cuttings provide excellent intelligence in this respect, allowing the community relations team to identify the principals in any protest and communicate with them directly. They have also found that early engagement with local media, prior to the planning application being submitted, can prevent reportage of a community protest becoming a newspaper-led campaign to prevent development.

Breaking down barriers

If physical barriers such as high walls, security gates, etc separate the organisation and the community, it is sensible to suggest that psychological barriers may result unless an effort is made by the organisation to prevent this.

To this effect, an organisation should be as open as possible. This can be done in a variety of ways. Open Days, for example, can be arranged where members of the public are invited to the plant and shown around, a talk can be given and refreshments supplied. Likewise, the organisation can be brought to the community, for example, through interactive mobile units manned by staff where members of the public are invited to learn more about the company. School trips to the plant can be arranged and talks, for example on the environment, can be given at local schools. Work experience can also be arranged. On a day-to-day basis, the company can also have a general open policy where people can phone ahead to be shown around the plant.

Literature such as leaflets, organisational community newsletters, etc. can be developed to supplement, not substitute, an ongoing two-way programme of communications with the community.

Handling complaints

Should members of the community complain to the organisation about any aspect of its functioning, this should be taken seriously and handled with care. For each person that complains there are many more with concerns who have not complained. If the organisation does not deal with the community's concerns, it increases the risk of organised resistance developing. Organisations should have a written procedure for handling complaints. An example of such a standard operating procedure is outlined below:

- All complaints should be handled by those responsible for community relations.
- These individuals should be available, day and night, to listen to concerns of local residents (by telephone out of normal working hours).
- Concerns should never be dismissed – they should be listened to, investigated and responded to in person at the earliest possible convenience.
- If action is required, it should be taken (if it is within the company's power).
- An explanation of the problem, an action plan and the time-frame involved should be explained to the community.
- All complaints should be documented.

Documenting complaints helps to identify emerging issues so they can be addressed sooner rather than later. It may also be a regulatory requirement for some companies.

Interaction between employees and the community

There is a close association between employees and the community as many employees may live in or have friends or family living in the local community. As a result, information flows to and fro between the community and the organisation on an ongoing basis. To help ensure that members of staff portray a realistic reflection of the company, they should be well educated on the organisation, its compliance with regulations and its commitment to reducing risk. Special attention should be paid to this area as part of ongoing staff training and induction courses for new employees. In addition, staff members should be encouraged, though not forced, to take an active part in community relations programmes.

The importance of risk communications

Risk communications as discussed in Chapter 8 are particularly important in the case of local residents whose fears are likely to be magnified by the proximity of the organisation and their lack of understanding of its activities. The following are important:

- allaying concerns by listening;
- recognising fears as legitimate and seeking to put them into perspective;
- creating an understanding of possible risk;
- reassuring on steps the organisation takes to prevent emergencies;
- reassuring on steps that will be taken in the event of such an emergency – including contacting residents immediately.

Communicating in emergencies

Trying to pretend to local residents that an emergency is not happening is next to impossible. They are not blind, deaf and certainly not dumb. They may see clouds of smoke, which may be harmless but they will think the worst – for their own protection. They may see a stream of ambulances and fire engines, which may be arriving to deal with a very small incident (emergency services usually overreact to accidents in chemical plants, for example) but residents will worry about what might have occurred and its likely implications. They may hear a loud explosion or smell strong, unfamiliar odours. Whatever the emergency or however small, residents will think the worst. They will fear for their safety and that of their children. They will wonder whether or not they should evacuate. Not surprising then that silence from the company compounds the situation.

During an emergency, panicking residents expressing their fears to the media only serves to heighten public concern. In the aftermath, public recrimination may result from media accusations of insensitivity to the public by not keeping them informed. The fragile trust that may have been painstakingly built up with the community through ongoing relationship building is threatened.

In the event of an emergency, local community representatives should be contacted immediately to explain the situation and what action, if any, needs to be taken. A special telephone number for residents to call in the case of an emergency can be pre-arranged with community representatives. However, the existence of this number should supplement, not negate, the need for the organisation to inform the community proactively in the event of an emergency.

Liaison groups

If an organisation is based in an industrialised zone, an alternative to each company individually meeting with local residents is the establishment of an industry/community liaison group. This option can work particularly well in building community relations. Representatives from each company in the locality, or perhaps representatives of a certain type of industry that causes most concern (eg chemical and pharmaceutical companies) would jointly meet with local residents on a regular basis. The existence of the liaison group would not rule out meetings between an individual company and residents should specific company-related issues arise.

The impression of industry versus residents must be avoided. One way of doing this is by calling the group 'a community liaison group'. Eligibility for membership depends on being a member of the community, with organisations considered part of the community. The purpose of meetings is for the overall benefit of the community. Inclusion in regular meetings helps to reassure residents that their concerns are being recognised in a formal way and that attempts are being made to deal with these concerns. Other advantages with this arrangement include:

- it is very much a community-based approach;
- residents get to know all local organisations on a personal level;
- all members of the group are updated on the local situation;
- the overall reputation of local industry is improved as companies that are not the source of a problem can put pressure on those that are and may be denying it;
- industry and locals working together increases their lobbying power in relation to local government issues such as the quality of roads;
- it saves time.

Sponsorship

Local sponsorship provides an organisation with the opportunity to be seen not only as a good corporate citizen but also as involved in and committed to the local community. This helps the relationship-building process.

However, if sponsorship is not well managed, it may reap little reward and prove a constant drain on finances as the organisation simply responds to repeated uncoordinated requests.

To manage sponsorship and realise benefits, a proactive sponsorship programme can be established and a sponsorship committee appointed with a definite budget and quantifiable goals.

In deciding what to sponsor, committee members must be familiar with the local community and its genuine needs. At the same time they should be cognisant of the messages the organisation wishes to relay. Ideally, organisations should sponsor a small number of issues of high local or national importance with high impact and visibility. The company should not be afraid to highlight the sponsorship; however, it should avoid overdramatising it.

The following areas can prove worthwhile to sponsor:

- local enterprise, eg training days;
- education, eg computers for schools, health talks, etc;
- environmental initiatives, eg clean-up projects, tree-planting, upkeep of local greens;
- arts and culture, eg local library, galleries, statues, works of art.

Some organisations run 'community days' – once a year, staff down tools to spend the day helping the community with such activities as painting the local school. Community days have numerous benefits, such as:

- reinforcing the view that the organisation is part of the community;
- involving employees in community relations programmes;
- genuinely getting the job done with warmth, not just handing out cash;
- boosting staff and community morale;
- improving the environment around the organisation;
- stimulating relaxed communication with the community.

Sponsorship programmes can be developed in conjunction with other local organisations in a coordinated manner. Members of a joint sponsorship committee representing local industry pool resources to provide financial support for community initiatives in a formalised manner. This results in a sizeable sponsorship fund that can be distributed strategically for the maximum benefit of the community. This minimises the risk of companies either overlapping in sponsorship activities or competing against one another to impress community members.

Look to others for ideas

When seeking to embark on a campaign of sponsorship and community involvement, it can be useful to look to other companies for ideas. United Utilities and North West Water (a company within the United Utilities group) are involved in a host of community related activities such as:

- Participating in a mentoring programme to help young people and the long-term unemployed find jobs. Young employee volunteers mentor local young people to help them gain confidence, develop skills and increase their employability.
- Participating in a mentoring programme to educate black and Asian students about career options and successful job search strategies.
- Working in partnership to promote employability for visually impaired people through free seminars, individual interviews, specialist workshops and telephone support to help educate on opportunities for study, training and work.
- Helping disaffected teenagers about to cease schooling through a learning programme linked to the workplace. Ten teenagers spend one day a week at one of NWW's Environmental Education centres to learn key skills, improving their chances of employment.
- Encouraging citizenship among young people. This involves a project aimed at putting the subject of citizenship on the agenda of local primary schools. This is a pilot for a national project.
- Participating in a campaign to improve the representation and contribution of women in the workplace.
- Providing £50,000 towards the refurbishment of a building in a local estuary designated a Special Protection Area and a Wetland of International Importance. The building was converted into a 'Discovery Centre' managed in a partnership between the Royal Society for the Protection of Birds (RSPB), the local borough council and NWW. It includes a visitor facility, a classroom for visiting school parties, a shop selling RSPB goods and

a separate room for NWW exhibition and interactive displays. Full-time staff are funded jointly by RSPB and NWW and NWW's educational staff regularly visit the classroom to get involved. Schoolchildren visit the centre to learn about the water cycle as part of their National Curriculum.

- Providing telescopes at one of NWW's reservoirs for people to view a pair of resident golden eagles.
- Each year, NWW employees take part in an event whereby they give their own time to help give people with disabilities the opportunity to try activities and events (eg canoeing) that might not normally be available to them.
- NWW has converted a derelict barn into a two-storey studio complex with an exhibition gallery and six work studios for newly qualified artists, sculptors and designers. NWW provides this facility rent-free for two years in return for artists donating ten hours per week of their own time to organise and run art clubs and events free of charge for the community.
- NWW sponsors a competition to promote conservation, access and recreation, and environmental education initiatives on its land. This is open to all sections of the community. Entrants design a project (that should not exceed £20,000 to implement) that allows the company to improve its facilities under a theme, eg 'Disabled Initiatives'. NWW implements winning entries.

SUMMARY

- Community groups that pressure organisations become activists.
- Because they have very real concerns about their health and lifestyles they can prove to be committed, determined and powerful activists.
- Communities not only pressure organisations already present but also are particularly active at trying to prevent new organisations locating in their area.
- To be effective, management must be committed to community relations.
- Ongoing, two-way symmetrical communications should be employed in a similar way to dealing with activists. However, special attention should be paid to:

-   the tone of communications;
-   how complaints are handled;
-   employee interaction with the community;
-   communicating about possible risks;
-   communicating in emergencies;
-   the benefits of liaison groups;
-   sponsorship.
- Liaison groups between local industry and residents provide a more community-based approach rather than each company working independently. However, genuine cooperation must exist.
- Sponsorship needs to be planned and controlled to avoid being a drain on resources.

10

Media relations

The media's ability to influence public opinion makes them an important audience for organisations. If activists attack an organisation, it is beneficial to have the media and public familiar with the company viewing it as open, honest and genuinely addressing issues of concern. The media should also feel comfortable contacting the company for information so that its side of the story is also reported. This chapter deals with media relations, an ongoing process to build links with and influence the media and public positively towards the organisation.

THE BENEFITS OF MEDIA RELATIONS

Initiating relations with the media and maintaining them over the long term can help to place the organisation on a more solid footing in the event of an activist attack by helping to:

- present the organisation as open, honest, helpful and co-operative;
- build an increased understanding of the organisation and its activities;

- put any risks associated with organisational functioning into perspective, allaying fears and concerns;
- educate on organisational efforts to address issues of public concern;
- influence opinion positively toward the organisation;
- build relations with key media contacts so that the organisation will be contacted should any news stories emerge relating to it.

MEDIA RELATIONS ARE AN ONGOING PROCESS

As outlined in Chapter 2, influencing public opinion is not easy. It takes proactive, ongoing and continuous efforts over the long term, during periods of relative calm. Without this approach, it will be too late to try to influence public opinion positively towards the organisation after an activist attack has begun.

TWO-WAY INFORMATION FLOW NEEDED

Media relations go beyond simply disseminating information on the company. To be successful, it must be a two-way process where views and concerns are sought so that the organisation can communicate in the most relevant manner. Over time, relationships are developed with key journalists by being accessible, open and accurate and by demonstrating an understanding of the media.

KEY ELEMENTS OF A MEDIA RELATIONS PROGRAMME

Media relations should be approached in an organised manner. The following steps are appropriate:

1. identifying key media and journalists;
2. learning their job;
3. building relations;

4. embarking on risk communications;
5. preparing to deal with the media in the event of emergencies.

Identifying key media and journalists

To build media relations it is necessary to identify key media and key journalists. A list should be drawn up of all media that are likely to report on the organisation including national and local radio, television and newspapers as well as relevant specialist publications. There is a need to be familiar with all of the relevant media and their editorial policies.

A list of relevant journalists in these media should then be compiled, starting with specialist correspondents of relevance, for example environmental correspondents, social affairs correspondents, etc. News editors are also key as they have overall control of news stories published. They are also less mobile in the job market than correspondents and therefore likely to remain in their position of relevance in the long term. Media lists should be kept up to date at all times.

Learning about the media

One of the most important steps to take in building relations with the media is to learn to facilitate them in performing their job. In order to do this, it is essential to know how they work and what is important to them.

Accuracy

There is an absolute necessity, for example, to supply accurate information as the journalist's personal reputation and that of the publication are on the line. It is preferable to admit inability to answer a question and commit to finding out rather than guessing and risk making an error.

Speed

The media work to deadlines, usually short. If they ask for information they need it as soon as possible, if not immediately. If information cannot be supplied immediately, a journalist's deadline should be checked and the information supplied to meet this deadline with as much leeway as possible.

Timing

There are good and bad times in the day to contact the media, never as a news deadline approaches unless the information has been requested by a journalist, is urgent or cannot wait. For example, when contacting a radio newsroom with non-urgent material, it is advisable to do so as soon as possible after the last bulletin rather than in the immediate run-up to the next bulletin when journalists will be preparing to broadcast.

Simple messages

Organisations need to be aware that, regardless of the information they provide to the media, journalists can always take their own angle to a story. To minimise the risk of this occurring, information supplied should be newsworthy, clear and accurate. Ideally there should be no more than three main messages per communication. Expert quotes are important to the media, so providing access to such experts is appreciated. The importance of visual images for television and print media should also be kept in mind.

Public relations professionals specialise in media relations. If there is little in-house expertise in this area, consultants can be hired or relevant staff trained.

Building relations

Building relations with key media does not happen overnight – a planned, incremental approach is advised involving a programme of two-way symmetrical communications.

Personal contact should be made and maintained with key journalists, preferably in order of importance. This can be done in a variety of ways including one-to-one meetings, media events and ongoing day-to-day contact. High standards of communication should be set.

One-to-one meetings

One-to-one meetings are of value in building relations with key media because personal contact is made and time is allocated on both sides to communicate face-to-face. From the media point of view, one-to-one meetings provide:

● access to key personnel within an organisation;

- an opportunity to question in detail about a subject;
- an opportunity to develop a unique media story;
- an opportunity to build contacts should information be required in the future.

One-to-one meetings may involve an informal meeting with the managing director of an organisation. This may or may not take place over a meal and may or may not include the option of a follow-up tour of the organisation. It is important to keep in mind that a journalist's job is news and that he or she has limited time. Therefore, in addition to general communication on the organisation, it is advisable to offer a unique media story. The promise of an 'exclusive' may be necessary for the reporter to meet in the first place.

Prior to organising such meetings, it is necessary to decide what information the organisation wants to impart and what newsworthy angle can be offered. It is also necessary to consider and prepare answers for any questions the journalist may ask. These may be based on the reputation of the organisation and/or recent news stories relating to it.

Media events

Organising events for the media as a group has the benefit of getting messages across to a wide group in a limited time period while providing the press with newsworthy material. Media events include press conferences, seminars, open days involving company announcements such as expansion plans, etc. As these events typically involve dissemination of information with limited opportunity for two-way communication, they should not take the place of one-to-one briefings; rather they should supplement them.

Day-to-day interaction

To maintain good relations and ensure the credibility of the organisation, efforts should be made to ensure the quality of information released to the media. For example, press releases should:

- be newsworthy, accurate and to the point;
- present as news rather than promotional blurb;
- include a newsworthy quote;
- be dated correctly;
- contain contact details.

In handling queries, information supplied should be accurate and complete. Queries should be handled immediately whenever possible. If this is not possible, the journalist's deadline should be checked, and the information provided to meet this deadline.

Risk communications

Risk communications (as outlined in Chapter 8) should be employed with media contacts once a relationship has been established and the journalist can be trusted not to misrepresent the information. Risk communications should occur during one-to-one meetings at a time when the organisation is not coming under public scrutiny or pressure. Care should always be taken to put risks into perspective so as to avoid panic stories emerging.

Emergencies

In an emergency it is unrealistic to expect media contacts to be biased towards the company. However, if good media relations exist, the media should have a better understanding of the company to start with. They should see it as open and not afraid to talk about the risks associated with its business. They should be aware of the steps taken by the company to avoid risks and that an emergency programme had been prepared. They are likely to have greater trust in company statements and confidence in quotes provided and feel confident in approaching the organisation directly before approaching third parties.

Communicating in an emergency is dealt with in Chapter 11.

SUMMARY

- Long-term, proactive media relations can help to place the organisation in a better position in the eyes of the media and public in the event of an activist attack.
- Influencing opinion is very difficult. Media relations should be an ongoing process that ideally begins before opinion has been formed on the organisation.
- Media relations involve a process of two-way symmetrical communications.

- Planning is essential. The following steps are suggested:
  - identifying key media and journalists;
  - learning about the media;
  - building long-term, ongoing relations with key media;
  - embarking on risk communications with appropriate contacts;
  - preparing to deal with the media in emergencies.

11

Emergencies

Organisational emergencies such as oil spills, explosions, chemical leaks, etc attract activist condemnation. Activists can also create emergencies for organisations by targeting them through, for example, orchestrated media campaigns.

Emergencies and the way they are handled put an organisation's reputation well and truly on the line. It is as if the world stops in silence, all eyes focused on the organisation and its desperate efforts to cope. It is public scrutiny at its worst. The media adopt the role of jury and executioner questioning the organisation's ability, integrity, efficiency, concern, openness, etc. Suddenly the organisation is plunged into a defensive situation that threatens its reputation, sales, profits, share price, staff motivation, jobs and stability (takeover may become a possibility). In this chapter we deal with sudden emergencies involving activists.

WHY ACTIVISTS LOVE EMERGENCIES

For activists, the word 'emergency' equals opportunity as:

● Emergencies create a media platform to highlight wider issues.

A chemical spill, for example, provides an opportunity for environmentalists to use the ensuing media interest and public concern to call for stricter controls on chemical plants.

- Emergencies attract media attention offering activists the opportunity to increase their profile, influence public opinion and attract new members and funding.
- Emergencies can inject new life into jaded issues. An accident at a nuclear plant, for example, awakens fresh concerns for safety and renewed media interest.
- Organisations coping with an emergency such as an explosion are often slow to respond to media scrutiny or do so ineffectively, leaving journalists desperate for comment. This provides an immediate news gap for activists' well-thought-out, emotional sound bites.
- Activists, who usually have to create an event to get news, do not have to invest resources and energy in 'selling a story' to the media – everything has been done for them and the media are all ears.

PREVENTION IS PREFERABLE

Because activists have so much to gain from emergencies and because they tend to mistrust organisations, they are unlikely to be persuaded from dramatising the issue. This is why long-term, proactive, ongoing relationship building with activists is so important to help prevent activist attacks and to ensure that, should organisational emergencies occur, activists appreciate the organisation's situation.

Take, for example, the hypothetical case of an environmental group that has built up a good long-term relationship with a chemical manufacturer, with both sides genuinely working together to lessen the company's environmental impact. Progress has been made and plans are in place to make further improvements. An accident occurs. The environmental group has to weigh up the pros of short-term publicity against the cons of damaging a working relationship that is resulting in environmental progress. Rather than jumping on the bandwagon in openly criticising the organisation, they may remain silent or more realistically they may temper their comments, eg focus on general issues rather than on the company *per se*.

Other activities that help organisations withstand emergencies are ongoing programmes involving risk communications (Chapter 8), media relations (Chapter 10), community relations (Chapter 9) and crisis preparation and planning (see below). These activities help to build a more positive image of the organisation should an emergency occur.

CRISIS PREPARATION AND PLANNING

Emergencies invite pressure from activists, the media, government, regulatory bodies and general public. The organisation's reputation, staff morale, sales, share price, profitability, etc are under threat, not only in the short term but well after the immediate crisis is over. It is wise, therefore, to prepare for such events through crisis planning and preparation. In brief, this involves:

- developing an exhaustive list of all the possible crises that may occur;
- selecting and appointing a crisis management team of top management from relevant speciality areas;
- drawing up a written crisis management plan outlining procedures in the event of all of the listed crises;
- selecting and preparing a crisis management centre for all activities to be focused in the event of a crisis;
- allocating a nearby room for media activities;
- selecting and training a credible media spokesperson, such as the chairperson or chief executive, in the media;
- appointing and training a stand-in in the event of absence;
- preparing a media pack with up-to-date and relevant background details on the organisation for immediate release in the early stages of an emergency;
- conducting regular dry runs of various crisis scenarios;
- crisis management consultants can be hired to coordinate a crisis management programme and to train staff on crisis issues.

WHAT TO DO IN THE EVENT OF AN EMERGENCY

If an emergency occurs:

- There will be an immediate news gap that needs to be filled. If the organisation does not confidently and quickly take control of the situation by implementing the crisis plan and supplying accurate information as soon as it is available, the media will increasingly seek comment from third parties such as activists.
- The organisational message should be decided upon without delay. It should be simple, clear, easily understood and reinforced by repetition. In trying to simplify complex or technical areas, care must be taken to avoid misrepresenting the truth.
- It should be agreed that the dedicated media-trained spokesperson be the only one to speak to the media so that the message relayed is consistent and well presented. The organisation's position should be relayed to all members of staff without delay so that the company is thinking as a unit. Opinion leaders, regulatory agencies, trade bodies, etc also need to be kept informed. They are also likely to be questioned by the media. International headquarters must also be regularly updated as they will need to keep local offices up to speed in case the crisis becomes a global issue.
- The appointed spokesperson should be made available to the media immediately, sounding sympathetic yet in control, focusing on what is being done to resolve the situation, rather than speculating as to the cause of the emergency.
- The media need to be kept informed with regular, open and accurate updates. If bad news needs to be delivered, the organisation should do so and early. Otherwise it may be 'leaked' by others, allowing the organisation to lose control over its delivery. Care must be taken with certain sensitive information such as details of victims (families need to be informed first).
- Members of the local community are often those most worried and have most to lose. As outlined in Chapter 9, they should be informed of the situation immediately.
- An organisation should facilitate the media as much as possible. Media who visit the site of an emergency, for example, can be provided with information, office equipment

to write up stories, refreshments, protective clothing and, if relevant, supervised tours. Photography and video footage can even be provided by the organisation.

- The Internet should not be ignored as it is a source of international, instant access to information.

SHOULD ACTIVISTS BE APPROACHED DURING EMERGENCIES?

If good relations exist

If an organisation experiencing an emergency has built up good, solid relationships with activist groups where trust exists, the advised approach is relatively clear-cut. The person responsible for dealing with activists should contact the groups immediately to explain the situation, what has occurred, the implications, what the organisation is doing about it and, if possible, what can be done in the future to prevent it reoccurring. Both sides can discuss what the activists intend to do. Negotiation may be needed to minimise negative outcomes.

This course of action is based on:

- a trust existing between the organisation and the group and a desire on both sides to maintain the mutually beneficial relationship;
- activists being tempted to comment to the media on the crisis – they will need to be given good reason not to;
- activist groups communicating with one another – groups may influence one another positively;
- while activist groups are unlikely to talk positively to the media about the organisation, they may decline to comment negatively.

If no relations exist

The situation where no relations have been built with activist groups is less clear-cut. The organisation is at a distinct disadvantage as the groups are likely to be critical, suspicious and even hostile. They are unlikely to want to talk to the organisation because of these feelings and also because they see numerous advantages in speaking to the media.

If the organisation decides not to open a dialogue with the activists, it should expect criticism. On the other hand, if the organisation decides to approach activists, it risks revealing sensitive information that can be used against the company. Neither situation is ideal. The following may prove helpful in deciding whether or not to approach activists during emergencies.

Past experience

If activists have been uncooperative in the past, it can be assumed that they are unlikely to cooperate in an emergency.

Non-activist-generated emergency

In the case of an emergency that has not been generated by activists (eg a chemical spill), it may be advisable to postpone communication with groups until the media frenzy has died down. Activists are unlikely to trust the organisation or its arguments and may use sensitive information provided by the organisation against it. For reasons outlined earlier, there will be an enormous temptation for groups to talk to the media. It will be difficult to stop them from doing so, especially if there is no existing relationship between the two.

In deciding to postpone communications with activists, the organisation needs to take firm control of media handling as described earlier. Media comment from activists should also be closely monitored and once the initial frenzy has abated, a cautious two-way symmetrical programme of communications should begin.

Activist-generated emergency

While each situation is different and generalisation is difficult, in the case of an activist-generated emergency (ie, an activist attack independent of organisational emergencies), it may be advisable to speak with groups on the basis that:

- they have a specific problem with the organisation, enough to take action;
- this problem is encouraging them to seek third-party involvement;
- ignoring activists is likely to be seen as ignoring public concern;

- ignoring activists encourages the situation to spiral out of control as described in Chapter 2.

The exception to this approach would be hostile, militant groups that consistently take an uncooperative stance. Dealing with such groups is addressed in Chapter 7.

Activists contacting the organisation

Should activists want to talk with the organisation during an emergency, a meeting should be set up on the assumption that the group wants to listen to the organisation. While two-way symmetrical communications should be adopted, as the company is in crisis, thought needs to be given to information supplied in the short term.

IF APPROACHING ACTIVISTS IN AN EMERGENCY

Ultimately it is up to each individual organisation to decide the best approach based on its own circumstances and that of the group/s pressurising it. If a decision is taken to approach activists in an emergency, two-way symmetrical communications should be employed as outlined in Chapter 6. However, as the organisation is starting from a negative position, apologising for not responding to activist concerns sooner is important to start the relationship-building process. Also important is promising to work with them to improve the situation and avoiding the temptation to persuade. If activists refuse to meet the organisation, relevant audiences such as the media can be informed that attempts were made and rebutted.

SUMMARY

- Emergencies either created or worsened by activist pressure threaten an organisation's reputation, sales, profits, share price, staff motivation, etc. A takeover may become a possibility.
- Activists love emergencies because they present a media platform to highlight bigger issues. Extensive media exposure

helps to increase their profile, attracting new members and funding. Jaded issues can be rejuvenated. Organisations, taken unawares, are usually slow or inadequate in their response.

- Because emergencies offer such opportunities to activists and because they do not trust organisations, they are unlikely to be persuaded from getting involved unless an existing relationship has been built up between both sides through ongoing two-way symmetrical communications.

- Crisis preparation and planning help organisations prepare for emergencies. Crisis management consultants can help organisations develop an expertise in this area.

- An organisation that has built good relations with activists should contact them in the event of an emergency to explain the situation and to negotiate on minimising any negative involvement they may be considering.

- An organisation is at a disadvantage if no relations exist, as groups are unlikely to trust it and will see numerous benefits in talking to the media. It is up to the organisation to decide whether or not to approach groups in this situation and the following may be taken into consideration when making that decision:

  - If no approaches are made, criticism should be expected. Effective and speedy media activities are required.

  - If approaches are made, activists may use sensitive information divulged against the organisation.

  - If activists have been uncooperative in the past they are unlikely to cooperate during an emergency.

  - In a non-activist-generated emergency, communication may be put on hold until the initial crisis is under control.

  - In an activist-generated emergency there are benefits in talking with groups as long as they are not traditionally hostile and uncooperative.

  - Should activists contact the company to set up a meeting this should be arranged.

- If meeting with groups during an emergency, the organisation should adopt two-way symmetrical communications but should tread cautiously.

12

Planning and evaluation

At this stage, rather than sitting back in the comfortable belief that you know what to do, it is advisable to get straight to work by planning a proactive communications programme with inbuilt evaluation mechanisms for monitoring its effectiveness. This chapter deals with planning and evaluating two-way symmetrical programmes.

WHY PLAN AND EVALUATE?

The main purpose of planning and evaluation is to improve the relevance and effectiveness of campaigns. Planning and evaluating go hand in hand – planning identifies and sets the goals of the campaign, while evaluation assesses the attainment of these goals. Planning ensures that a coordinated plan of action is developed to maximise results for resources spent. Ongoing evaluation, initiated at the outset of a programme, helps to identify successful and unsuccessful activities allowing the campaign to be adapted early and proactively according to results. Programmes should be flexible enough to be altered on an ongoing basis according to results assessed through evaluation.

Planning and evaluation can also prove useful in situations where management may need to be reminded of the benefits of allocating resources to activism. Planning and evaluation help to identify the goals of the programme and the progress that is being made in attaining these goals.

THE MOST BASIC APPROACH: PUBLIC RELATIONS BY OBJECTIVES

Planning and evaluation need not be tedious. One of the most basic and sensible approaches is public relations by objectives. This involves setting realistic objectives at the planning stage of the programme. The attainment of these objectives is then measured on an ongoing basis as the programme is implemented to determine its success. It is therefore essential that, when setting objectives, there must be a way of measuring the attainment of each and every objective.

Objectives can be simple; the main caveat is that they are realistic and can be achieved ideally within the time-frame allocated. Non-attainment of objectives can be demotivating not only for those involved but also for management. To ensure that the momentum of the campaign is maintained, both short and long-term objectives should be set. For all objectives, deadlines should be specified. Longer-term objectives and their deadlines may be altered as the campaign progresses according to how the situation is developing. All objectives should be reviewed regularly to see if they are being met or if they need to be altered.

SETTING PROGRAMME OBJECTIVES

Overall objectives

When setting objectives, the overall aims of the programme need to be examined. A good place to begin is to look at the broad objectives of the various stages of two-way symmetrical programmes for dealing with activists, as follows:

1. appointing responsibility to a suitable candidate;
2. developing a thorough research programme;
3. negotiation, relationship building, conflict resolution, aiming for a win-win situation;
4. developing workable media relations, community relations and risk communication programmes;
5. developing a thorough crisis management plan.

Specific objectives

To focus objectives and ensure they are measurable, it is useful to categorise them according to their subject area; so, for example, there would be specific research objectives. Objectives will, of course, vary from organisation to organisation. However, as an exercise, examples are given below.

Objectives relating to appointing responsibility

Examples of objectives relating to appointing responsibility for dealing with activists could include:

- long term/overall:
  - ensure that the right people are doing the job.
- short term:
  - appoint by a certain date a suitable candidate with relevant qualifications;
  - select a support team of three, with complementary backgrounds and skills;
  - set up an ongoing training programme that identifies and satisfies the needs of the entire team;
  - establish structures for management involvement, eg monthly meetings.

Research objectives

Research objectives could include:

- long term/overall:
  - identify and keep in touch with the views of all activist groups that may prove a threat;
  - keep track of public opinion of the organisation and relevant general issues such as the environment;

- – ensure research results are useful and used in the formulation of communication plans.
- short term:
  - – develop by a certain date, a budgeted, strategic yet flexible research plan;
  - – appoint by a set date a research coordinator with suitable background and training;
  - – meet specified deadlines for the completion of research projects;
  - – stay within specified budgets;
  - – establish review mechanisms to keep the overall programme focused.

Relationship-building objectives

Objectives could include:

- long term/overall:
  - – take control of the threat of activism by being proactive;
  - – build relations with all groups regardless of size;
  - – reduce conflict.
- short term:
  - – obtain the support of management for two-way symmetrical communications;
  - – set a deadline for the first meeting with activists to take place;
  - – get activists to hedge their concerns with those of the organisation;
  - – genuinely work with activists;
  - – involve activists in relevant decision-making processes;
  - – document progress.

Media relations, community relations, risk communications

Possible objectives could include:

- long term/overall:
  - – build strong foundations for the organisation in the event of an activist attack;
  - – build relations with key audiences;
  - – build an understanding of the organisation, its activities and its efforts to be open, honest and accountable.

- short term:
  - develop a media relations plan, community relations plan and risk communications strategy;
  - appoint responsibility to relevant members of staff;
  - appoint a sponsorship committee and develop a sponsorship programme;
  - develop a written complaints procedure;
  - understand the workings of the media by a certain deadline;
  - hold a community day once a year.

Planning for emergencies

Objectives could include:

- long term/overall:
  - be prepared for any crisis both in terms of procedures and communications;
  - reassure relevant audiences of emergency plans.
- short term:
  - hire crisis management consultants;
  - develop a crisis management plan;
  - conduct regular dry runs.

SHORT- AND LONG-TERM EVALUATION

Ideally, to achieve an effective, relevant and proactive campaign, both short- and long-term evaluation[1] should be employed. Short-term evaluation is project based and covers periods of less than 12 months. It assesses the success rates of individual projects in an attempt to improve the relevance of future projects. Long-term evaluation is broader and more strategic, using public relations by objectives as outlined earlier in this chapter. Regular feedback from long-term evaluation helps to fine-tune programme planning and implementation.

---

[1] Noble, P G (1998) *Towards an Inclusive Evaluation Methodology*, paper at the Annual Conference of Public Relations Educators' Forum, Leeds Metropolitan University

EVALUATING SYMMETRICAL PROGRAMMES

Evaluation has traditionally focused on measuring persuasion. Now, as communicators realise the limitations of trying to persuade and change behaviour and attitudes, this measurement is becoming less important.[2] Measuring persuasion is also less relevant in symmetrical programmes, where the focus is primarily on negotiation and conflict resolution.

To evaluate symmetrical programmes, the 'co-orientation model'[3] is used. This examines the relationship between an organisation and activists. Applying this model, there are four possible 'co-orientation states' in the relationship between an organisation and activists. The first is a state of 'true consensus' where both sides share the same views and both are aware of this agreement. The second is the state of 'dissensus' where conflicting views are held and both sides are aware of the conflict. The third state is 'false consensus' where either party perceives agreement that is not there. The fourth state is 'false conflict' where either side perceives disagreement that does not exist. The co-orientation model helps an organisation to focus on the true condition of its relationship with activists so that effective communications programmes can be planned.

In order to identify the state of the relationship, primary research can be employed. Both the organisation and activists are surveyed. 'Agreement difference scores' are computed which show the gap in agreement between both sides. Accuracy difference scores are also computed to show the degree of accuracy in each party's view of the other's stance. Armed with the results of this research, objectives can be set to reduce agreement difference scores and accuracy difference scores between the parties. Reductions in agreement differences are key yardsticks of a programme's success where changes in the organisation's views are equally important as changes made by activists.

[2] Dozier, D and Ehling, W (1992) 'Evaluation of Public Relations Programs: What the literature tells us about their effects', in J E Grunig (ed), *Excellence in Public Relations and Communication Management*, Lawrence Erlbaum Associates, New Jersey
[3] Broom, G M and Dozier, D M (1992) *Using Research in Public Relations: Applications to program management*, Prentice-Hall, Englewood Cliffs, New Jersey

PREPARING COMMUNICATIONS PROGRAMMES

Setting objectives is just one part of communication programmes. Programme planning should also involve the development of a strategy toward the achievement of objectives. So, for example, an overall objective might be to reduce conflict with a group. A strategy would work out how this might be achieved, eg convincing the organisation's management to negotiate with activists; involving third-party arbitration between the organisation and activists; learning about and listening to groups, etc.

Once a strategy has been developed, a coordinated range of activities should be identified that will help to achieve this strategy. In the case outlined above these could include educating management about two-way symmetrical communications through case histories; six-weekly meetings with activists; regular meetings with management, etc. Brainstorming with other members of staff can prove useful in identifying a wide range of relevant activities.

At the outset, management should set aside a budget for the programme. Budgeting will involve a realistic estimation of cost for all individual activities, eg research costs, sponsorship, media relations expertise, crisis management expertise, etc.

A written document is then produced which clearly outlines the objectives, strategies and target audiences of the programme as well as the planned activities and a detailed budget. The timeframe for activities should also be set down. A calendar of events is a useful method for doing this. A written communications programme is essential in order to provide focus for those implementing it but also for management.

FULL STEAM AHEAD

Armed with a comprehensive programme and management support, the two-way symmetrical communications process can proceed full steam ahead.

Managing activism can be perceived as a major inconvenience or an exciting challenge. Knowing what to do and the fact that doing it increases the organisation's control and minimises the risk of surprise can help to make dealing with activists less of a nightmare. More positively, knowing that new and valuable skills will be acquired can turn learning to deal with activism into an exciting challenge and offer the opportunity to redefine one's role within the organisation.

SUMMARY

- Planning and evaluation help to focus communications programmes, increasing their relevance and effectiveness. Planning identifies and sets the goals of the campaign while evaluation assesses the attainment of these goals. This can prove valuable in reassuring sceptics of the benefits of allocating resources to activism.
- Public relations by objectives is a basic yet useful means of planning and evaluation. It simply involves setting realistic objectives at the start of a programme and then measuring the attainment of these objectives on an ongoing basis to determine its success. All objectives must be measurable and deadlines set for their attainment. All objectives need to be reviewed regularly to see if they are being met or if they need to be revised.
- Both short- and long-term evaluation should be employed. Short-term evaluation is project based and covers periods of less than 12 months. Long-term evaluation is broader and more strategic, using public relations by objectives.
- To evaluate symmetrical programmes, a special model that examines the relationship between an organisation and activists (the 'co-orientation model') can be used.
- While objectives form the basis of communications programmes, they need to be supplemented by a strategy and detailed list of planned, budgeted activities. A written communications programme is essential in order to provide focus for those implementing it and for management.

Further reading

Anderson, D S (1992) 'Identifying and Responding to Activist Publics: A case study', *Journal of Public Relations Research*, **4** (3), pp 151–65, Lawrence Erlbaum Associates, New Jersey

Broom, G M and Dozier, D M (1992) *Using Research in Public Relations: Applications to program management*, Prentice-Hall, Englewood Cliffs, New Jersey

Center, A H and Jackson, P (1995) *Public Relations Practices*, 5th edn, Prentice-Hall, New Jersey

Dozier D M *et al* (1995) *Managers' Guide to Excellence in Public Relations and Communication Management*, Lawrence Erlbaum Associates, New Jersey

Grunig, L (1992) 'Activism: How it limits the effectiveness of organizations and how excellent public relations departments respond', in J E Grunig (ed), *Excellence in Public Relations and Communication Management*, Lawrence Erlbaum Associates, New Jersey

Hager, N and Burton, B (1999) *Secrets and Lies: The anatomy of an anti-environmental PR campaign*, Craig Potton Publishing, Nelson, New Zealand

Sandman, P M (1993) *Responding to Community Outrage: Strategies for effective risk communication*, American Industrial Hygiene Association Press, Fairfax

Seymour, M and Moore, S (2000) *Effective Crisis Management*, Cassell, London

Vidal, J (1997) *McLibel: Burger culture on trial*, Pan Books, London

Wilcox, D L *et al* (1997) *Public Relations Strategies and Tactics*, 5th edn, Longman, New York

Index

preparation for activist pressure
48
OSPAR commission   1
outside influences, on organisations
62–63

persuasion   27, 143
  limitations, case study   39–42
Phillips and Drew   15, 16
planning and evaluation, two-way
  symmetrical programmes   39,
  138–39
Powerwatch   16–17
PR Consultants Scotland (PRCS)
  109
preparation, for activist attack   2, 48
Press for Change   24
press releases   127–28
proactive approach   35, 84
proactive strategies, *see also*
  relationship building
protection, from activist attack
  84–85
public, identifying potential activists
  58–59
public meetings   102, 114
public opinion   124
  influence by activists   9
  influence by targeted
    organisations   25
  and potential threats   54–61
  research into   55–56
public relations by objectives   139,
  145
public relations professionals   126

qualitative research   59–61
quantitative research   56–59
questionnaires   58

Rainforest Action Network (RAN)
  41
rainforests   30–31, 40–42
refusal to negotiate   82–85
relationship building   65
  objectives   141
  two-way symmetrical
    programmes   39
research   42
  into public opinion   55–56
  objectives   140–41

qualitative research   59–61
quantitative research   56–59
secondary research   60
two-way symmetrical programme
  38–39, 50–62
response to activist pressure   22–33
responsibility
  for activism   140
    choice of staff   44–45
    individual development   47
    support team   47
    training   45–46
  for community relations   112
risk
  dangers of non-communication
    93–94
  from activists   7–8
  perception gap   103
risk communications   93–99
  acceptance of fears   96
  apologising   96
  and community relations   114,
    116–17
  explanation   96–99
  key audiences   104
  listening to concerns   95
  and the media   128
  objectives   141–42
  Peter Sandman's questions
    105–06
  timing of commencement
    102–03
risk perception   105–06
Royal Forest and Bird Protection
  Society (F&B)   30
Royal Society for the Protection of
  Birds (RSPB)   120–21

'salami principle'   51
Sandman, Peter   97–98
  questions in risk communications
    105–06
Sandoz   10
Save our Shoreline   78
Schipol airport   15
scientific research   10
secondary research   60
secrecy   31–32
*Secrets and Lies: The anatomy of an
  anti-environmental PR campaign*
  31

151